**Contemporary
Art Station**

IRIS_FLUIDISM, works 2018-2024
Published by Contemporary Art Station

Publisher
ICM Gestora Cultural, SL
Paseo de Gracia 95, 5º-1ª
08008 Barcelona
Spain

ISBN: 978-84-10291-62-1
DL: GR 1270-2024

Library of Congress Cataloging-in-Publication Data
IRIS_FLUIDISM, works 2018-2024 / Contemporary Art Station.
Includes bibliographical references and index.
ISBN 978-84-10291-62-1

Printed in Spain, EU.

First Edition, 2024

Publisher's Contact Information:
Contemporary Art Station
contact@contemporaryartstation.com
www.contemporaryartstation.com

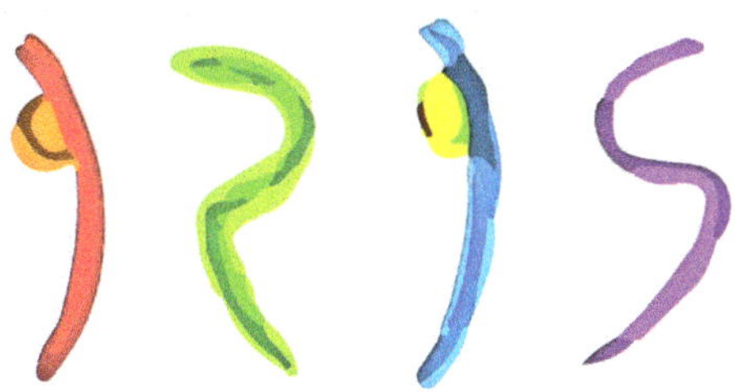

Contemporary
Art Station

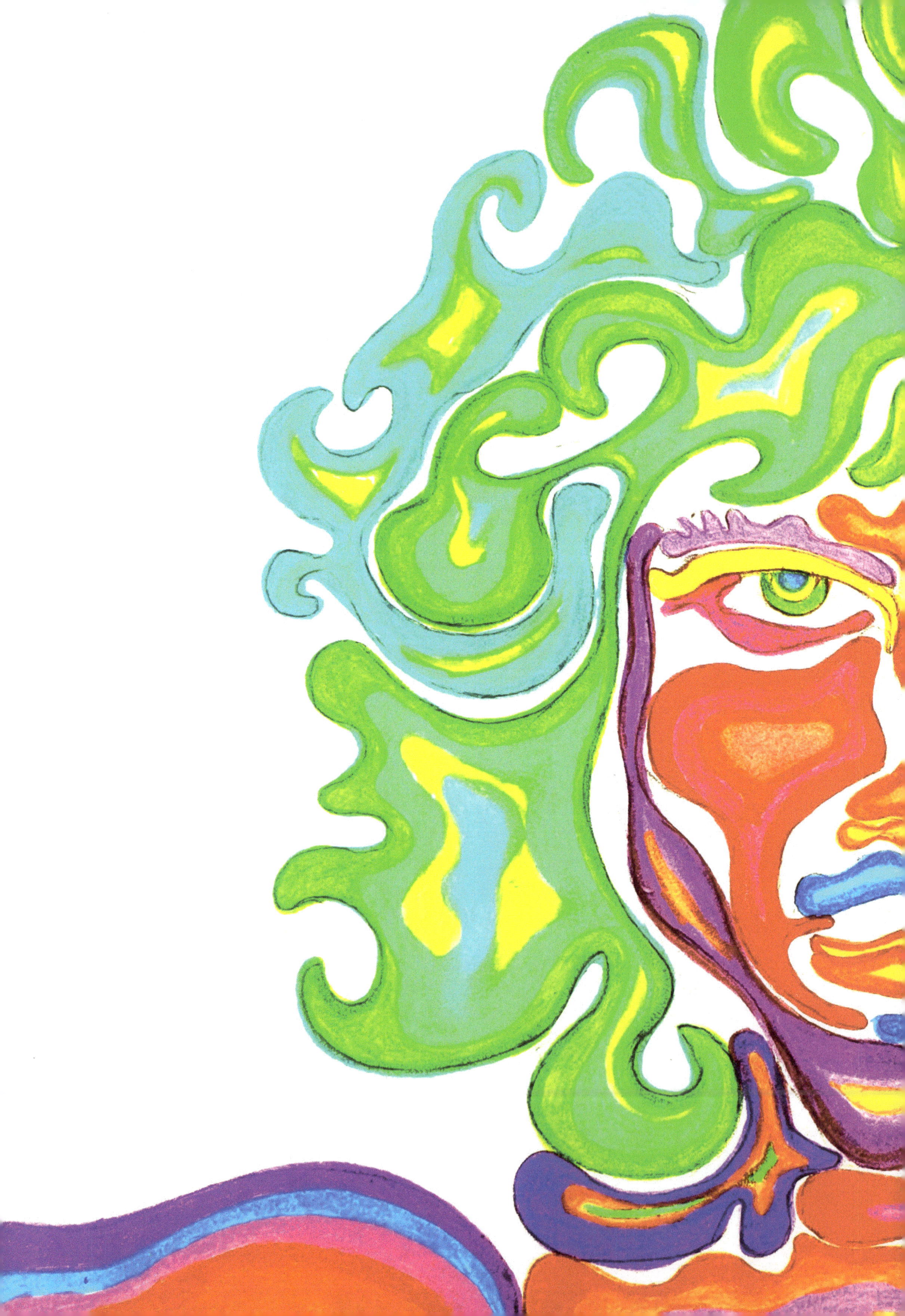

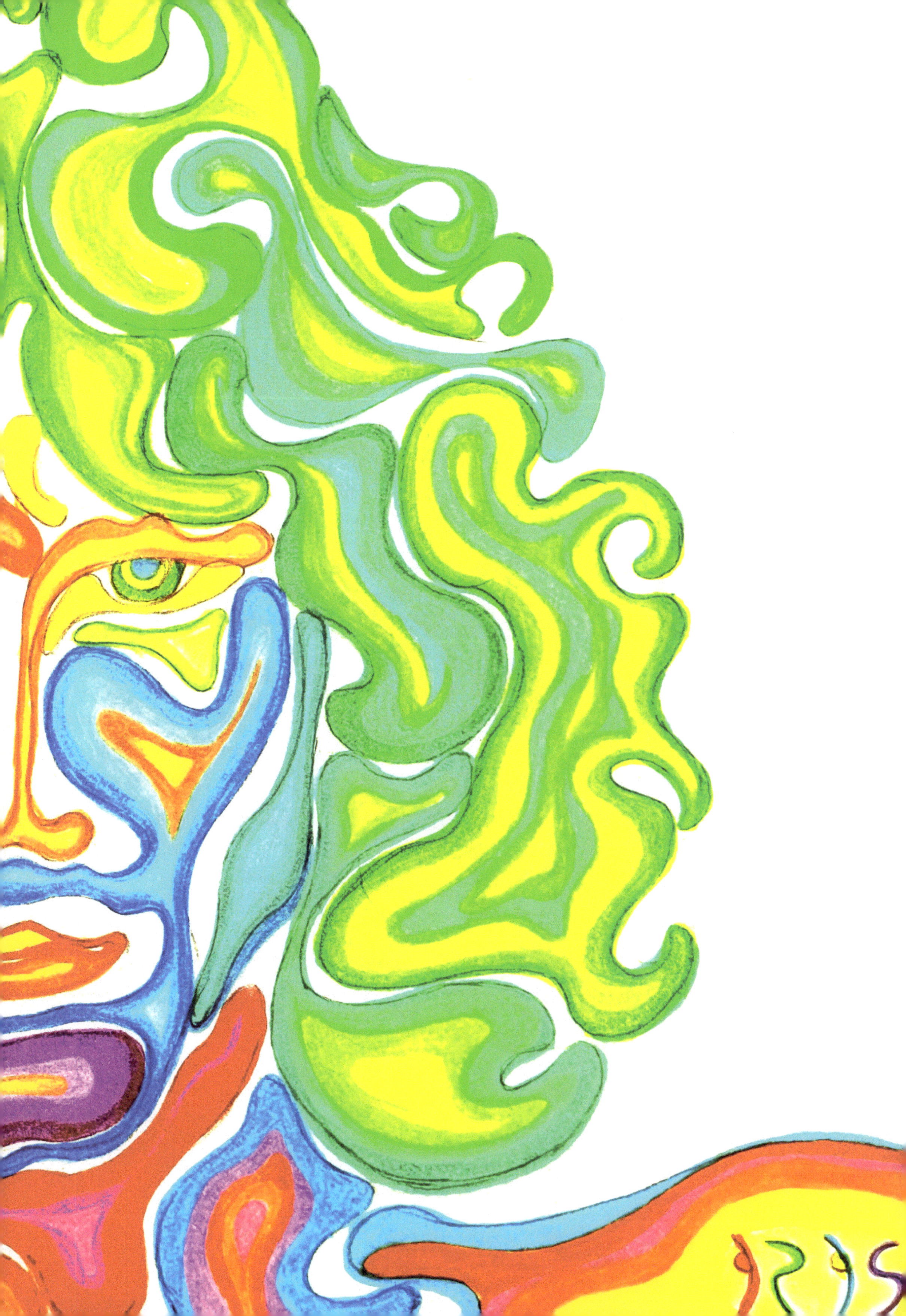

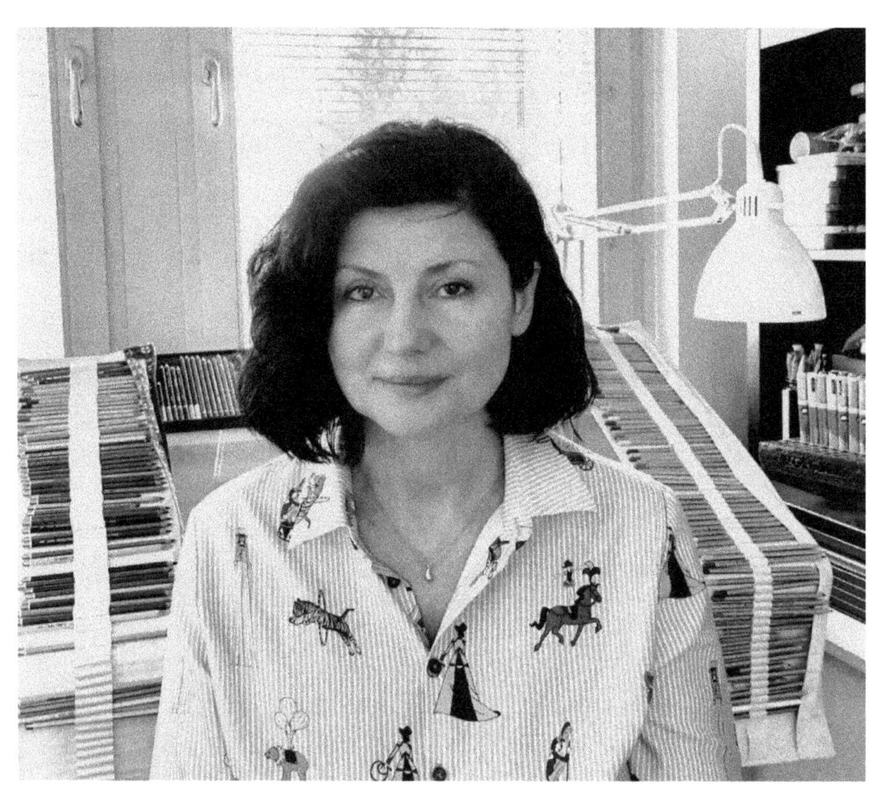

Biography

____

Carmen Rieger (IRIS) was born in Romania and has been living in Austria for almost 21 years. A graduate of the Faculty of Industrial Design she has worked for many years as a furniture designer. Since 2018 she has experienced a whole new style inspired by the organic forms that fluids create in their movement.

She called this new style "Fluidism".

For IRIS, her style Fluidism is a tribute to the most fascinating, important and complex fluid on Earth, without which life cannot exist _ WATER.

Water is witness to the interconnectedness and interdependence of all living things. For the artist, water is not only the flow of life, but also an expression of spirituality. It is a sacred gift of inestimable value that we must take care. For IRIS, water is an expression of love and interdependence of all life forms on the planet and in the Universe. Water unites all of creation into a whole of boundless beauty, diversity, and complexity. The water in our body reminds us of the beauty and the unique chance offered to be present in everyday life, to witness the magnificent spectacle of life.

Her artworks are composed of intricately organized, organic forms inspired by the movement of fluids. In the bodies of humans, plants and animals, water is found in a proportion of 70% or even higher. Thus, in the summer of 2018, IRIS had the idea of drawing only the liquid part of the bodies without completely destroying their original shape and character. In a person's portrait, for example, their character and inner life can be recognized. An elephant is transformed into a new elephant through a complex ensemble of colors and organic shapes without losing the idea of an elephant. A bird remains a bird without losing the idea of flight.

From the beginning, the artist chose to use the 7 colors of the rainbow and the shades obtained by combining them in all her works of art.

She wants to bring beauty, hope and love to life through her art.

____

FLUIDISM is the most important moment in my artistic career.
It is the essence of what I am. It is all about fluidity.

Everything flows.
Fluidity belongs to the human being,
is in our biological composition and in the composition of
our society in which we all are immersed. It is about a strong communication
system with its own language and infinite ways of expression.
It is about a reality that finds and elaborates its nature in
the liquid state of things.
We are immersed in it and we are carried
away by the flow of eternal becoming.

FLUIDISM is a concept through which I express
my artistic creed in works of art,
inspired by the existence of a complex substance of outstanding
properties and qualities – WATER.

WATER is a unique and indestructible substance.
WATER is the basis of life, growth and change.
WATER has the ability to regenerate continually.
WATER soothes and heals.
WATER shows understanding and sensitivity.

WATER is an accomplished artist. WATER is the most important element on the planet,
can be found in 70% of our earth and in the same proportion in the bodies of humans,
animals and plants – sometimes even in a larger quantity.
I have chosen to use the seven colors of the rainbow
and the shades obtained by combining them in all of my artworks.

I.R.I.S_ Individual Running Images of the Spectrum

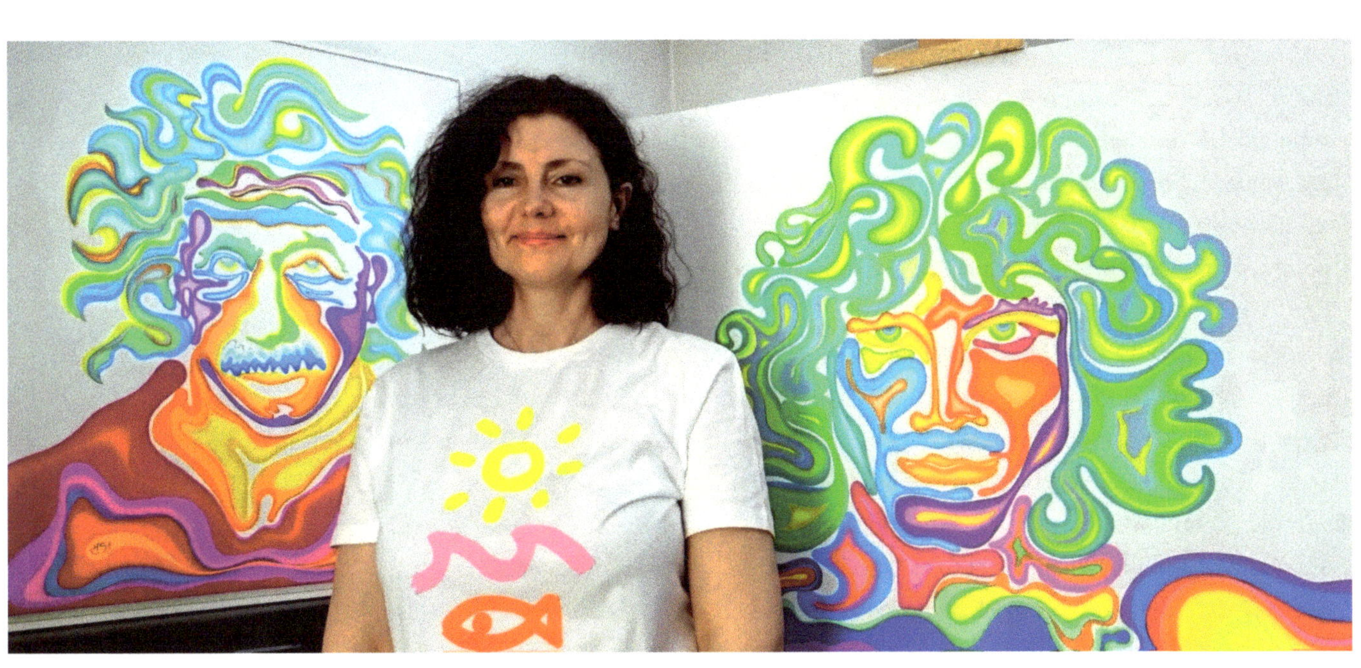

Art Fairs & Exhibitions

What Is Art First Edition Boomer Gallery London UK 4 December 2020

What Is Art Second Edition Boomer Gallery London UK 16-22 April 2021

Incandescent Madrid Spain 26 January - 4 February 2022 by Capital Culture House & EKA & Moor Gallery

Venice International Art Fair 2022 15th Edition Palazzo Bembo Palazzo Albrizzi-Capello Venice Italy
9-30 September by Itsliquid Group

Contemporary Venice 11th Edition 2022 Palazzo Bembo Venice Italy 20 October - 10 November by Itsliquid Group

Brain Cake Casa Mila "La Pedrera" Gaudi Room 28 December Barcelona Spain by Mads Art Gallery

Tokyo Tower Art Fair 2023 10 11 & 12 March 2023 Tokyo Tower Tokyo Japan by Contemporary Art Collectors

Beyond Utopia: Visions of a Perfect World June 15 - September 15 2023 by Contemporary Art Collectors

Contemporary Art Cannes Biennale Cannes France 19 May 2023 by MAMAG Modern Art Museum

Parallel Worlds by Contemporary Art Curator Magazine September 20 2023 - February 20 2024

Sanremo Biennale Theater Ariston Sanremo 14-17 September 2023

Segnalati Maltese Parliament Malta 6-23 October 2023 by Effetto Arte Fundation

Leaders Protagonists of Art at Washington Hilton Washington DC Capitol Hill USA November 2023 by Effetto Arte Fundation

Artist of the Week by Contemporary Art Collectors 25-31 December 2023

Mantua Biennale Diocesan Museum Francesco Gonzaga Mantua Italy 26 May - 9 June 2024 by Effetto Arte Fundation

Onboart Exhibition by Contemporary Art Station and Vueling Airlines, July 1-31, 2024

Infinity Exhibition by Florence Contemporary Gallery, June 2024

Continuity: Modern and Contemporary Masters Exhibition by Artifact Projects NYC Gallery, October 23 - November 2, 2024

Awards

Collectors Art Prize International Art Award 2023 March 31 2023 by Contemporary Art Curator Magazine
in collaboration with Contemporary Art Collectors platform
International Prize Pegasus for the Arts Scuola Grande di San Teodoro Venice Italy May 18 2023 by Effetto Arte Fundation
International Art Prize Michelangelo Teatro Italia Rome Italy July 22 2023 by Effetto Arte Fundation
International Art Prize Star of Art and Market Teatro Italia Rome Italy July 22 2023 by Effetto Arte Fundation
Harmony for Humanity: The Global Consciousness Art Prize August 12 2023 by Contemporary Art Collectors
Career Art Award 2023 Casino Theater of Sanremo September 16 2023 by Effetto Arte Fundation
International Art Prize Botticelli Borghese Palace Florence Italy January 20 2024 by Effetto Arte Fundation
Ambassador of Art 2024 Borghese Palace Florence Italy January 20 2024 by Effetto Arte Fundation
Global Art Virtuoso: Elite Artistic Career Achievement Award February 21 2024 by Contemporary Art Collectors
The Premier Artist Prize 2024 by Contemporary Art Station, June 4, 2024
The Future of Art Global Masterpiece Award by Contemporary Art Curator Magazine, July 20, 2024

Publications

____

Lights for the Future Corriere dell Arte 2020

Art Anthology III Guto Ajayu Culture Madrid October 2021

House and Garden UK April May June issues 2022

The World of Interiors May June July issues 2022

Chelsea Life (The Life Magazines) April May issues 2022

St. John's Wood Life on the back cover June issue 2022

Art Anthology V Guto Ajayu Culture Madrid July 2022

Art in America Annual Guide 40th anniversary edition by Artifact NYC Gallery 2023

ArteryNYC Magazine interview with Mr. Paul Zimmerman February 6 2023

Chelsea Life (The Life Magazines) August issue 2023

Contemporary Art Collectors Art Book by Contemporary Art Collectors August 16 2023

Chelsea Life (The Life Magazines) on the back cover December issue 2023

Top Contemporary Artists to Watch in 2024 by Contemporary Art Curator Magazine January 2024

Contemporary Art Curator Magazine art review by Ms. Marta Puig Editor of Contemporary Art Curator
Magazine December 2023

ArteryNYC Magazine art review by Mr. John Austin January 2024

55 Artists to Discover 2024 Edition March 2024 by Florence Contemporary Gallery

The Luxury Collection of Contemporary Artistry March 2024 by Contemporary Art Collectors Magazine

Vogue Manhattan New Faces April 2024

2025 Visionaries: Artists Shaping The Future. Creative Catalysts for Change by Contemporary Art Curator
Magazine, May 16, 2024

The Premier Artist Prize 2024 Book by Contemporary Art Station

Future of Art Global Masterpiece Award Art Catalog by Contemporary Art Curator Magazine, September 2024

ARTnews Top 200 Collectors Special September Edition, 2024

IRIS
FLUI
DISM
works
2018
2024

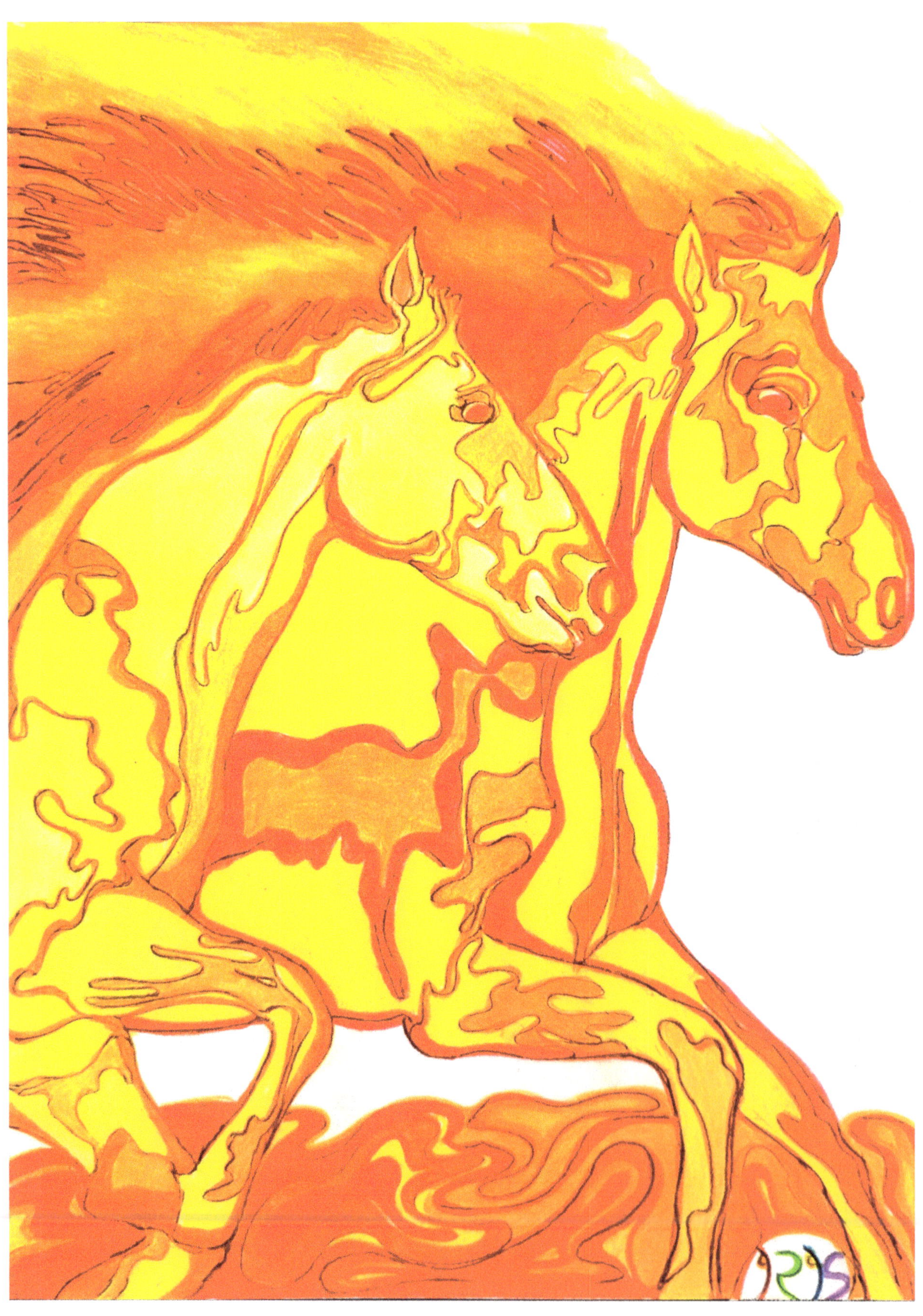

The Gallop of Hope, Passion and Freedom. Color pencils. 30x21cm. 2024

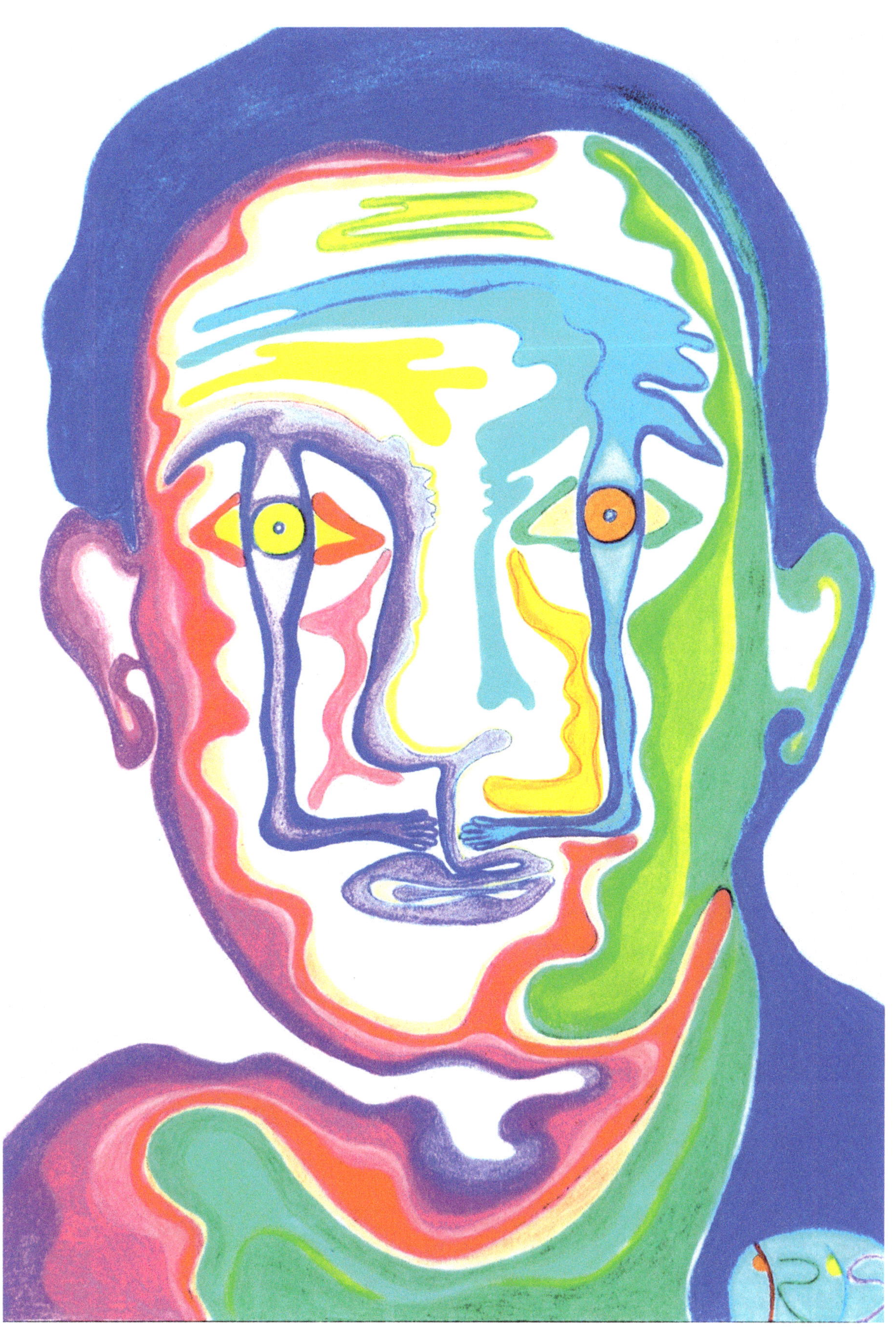

Salvador Dali. Color pencils. 30x21cm. 2024

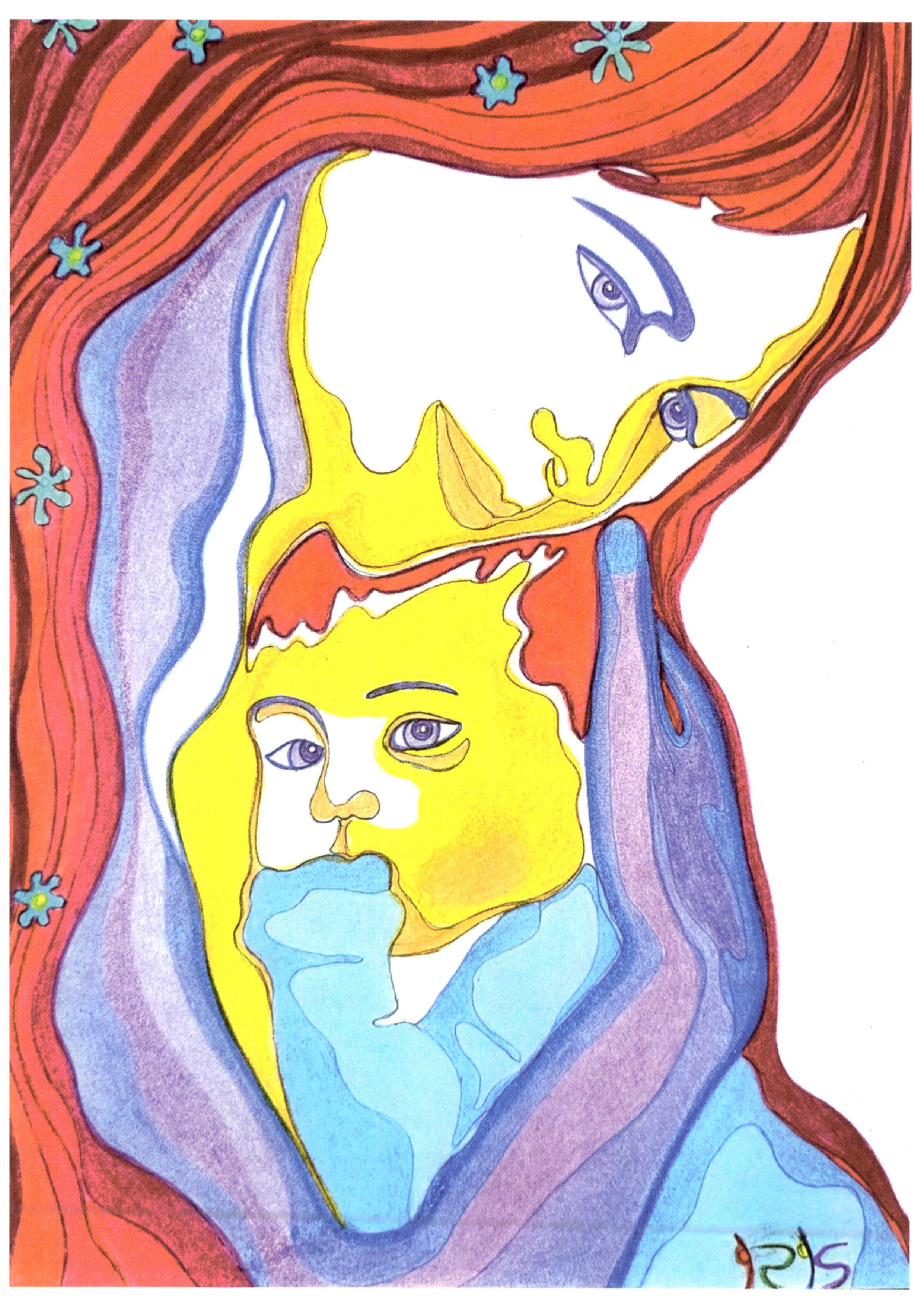

Love. Color pencils. 30x21cm. 2024

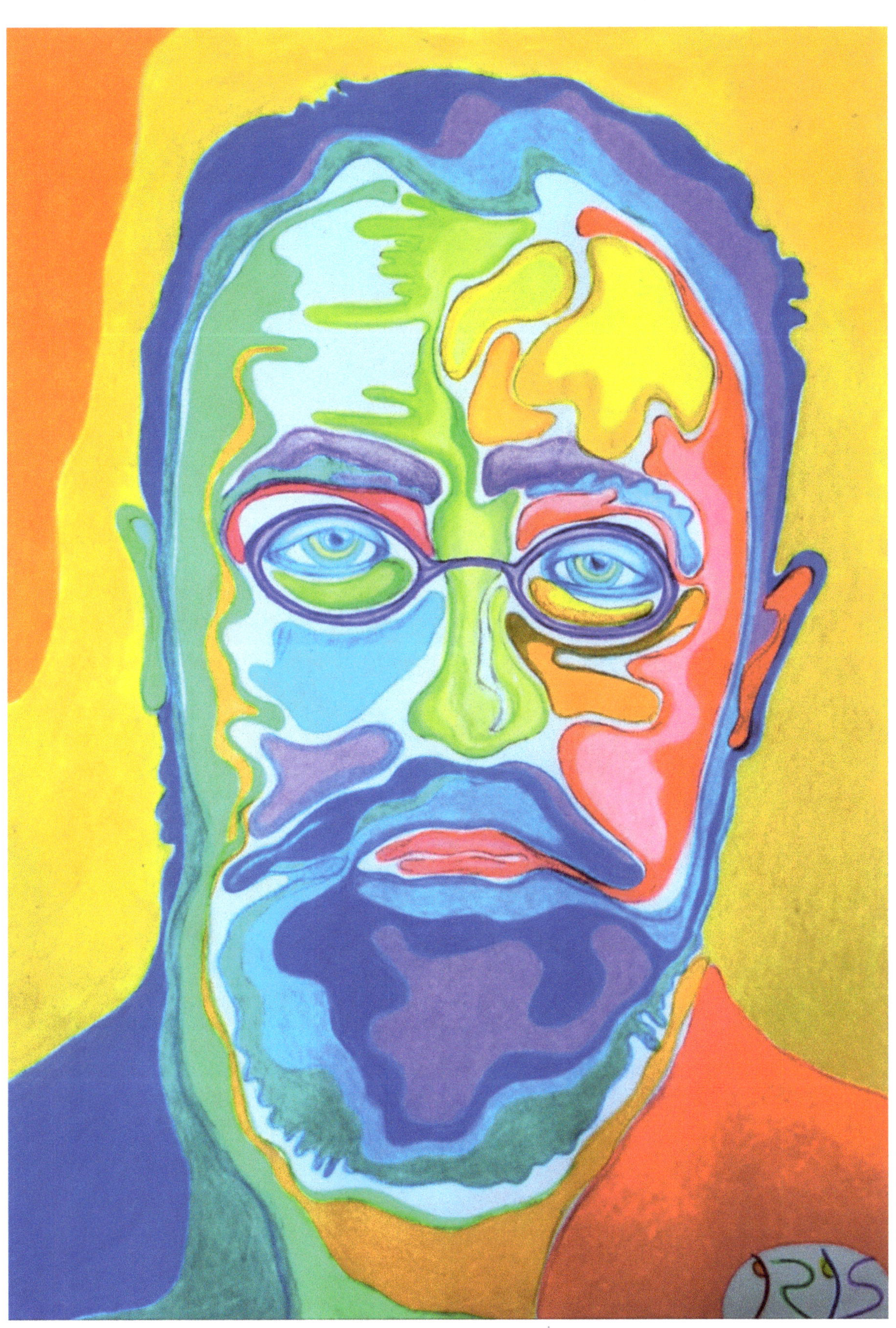

Henri Matisse. Color pencils. 30x21cm. 2024

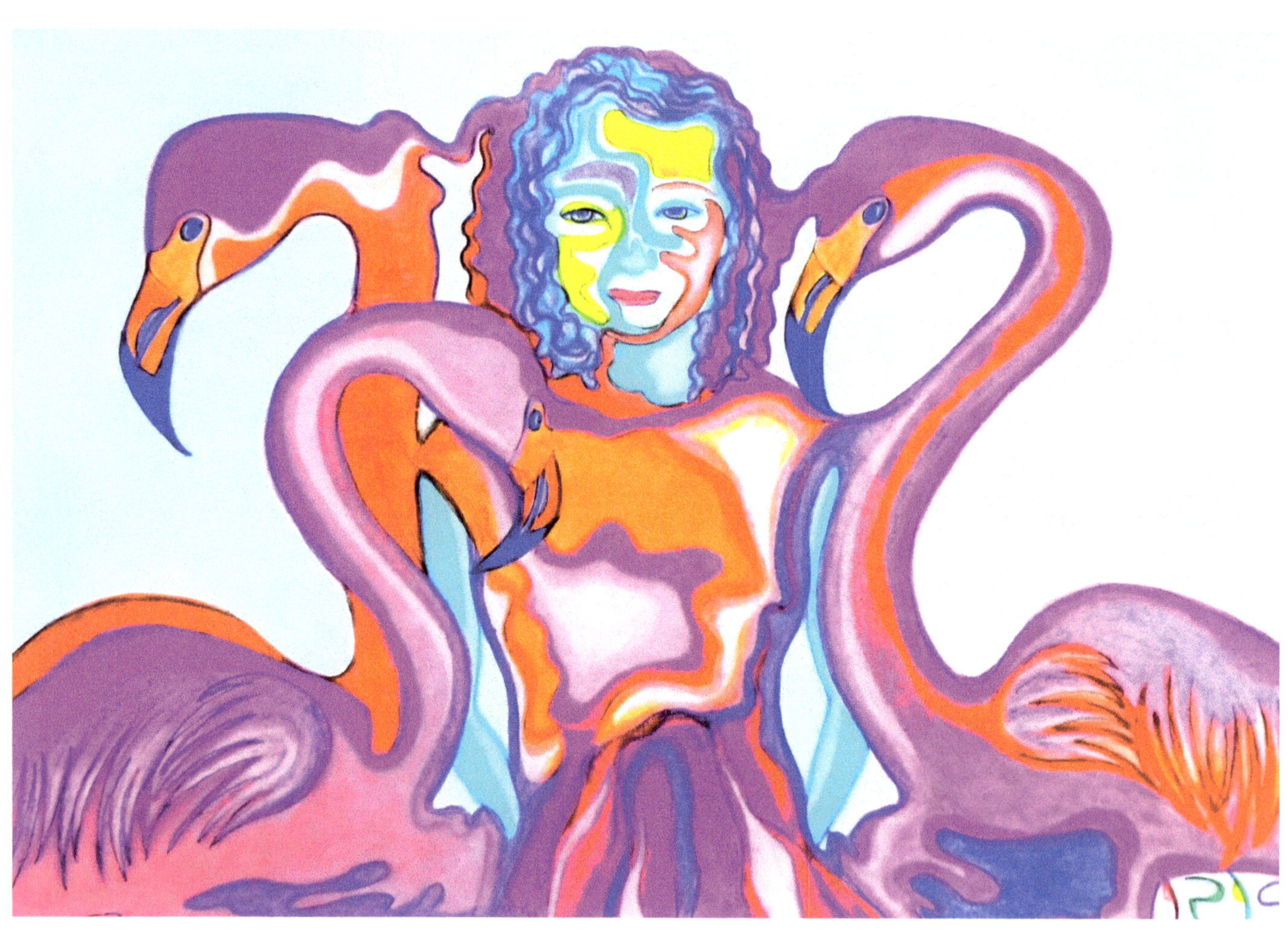

Symphony in Pink. Color pencils. 30x21cm. 2024

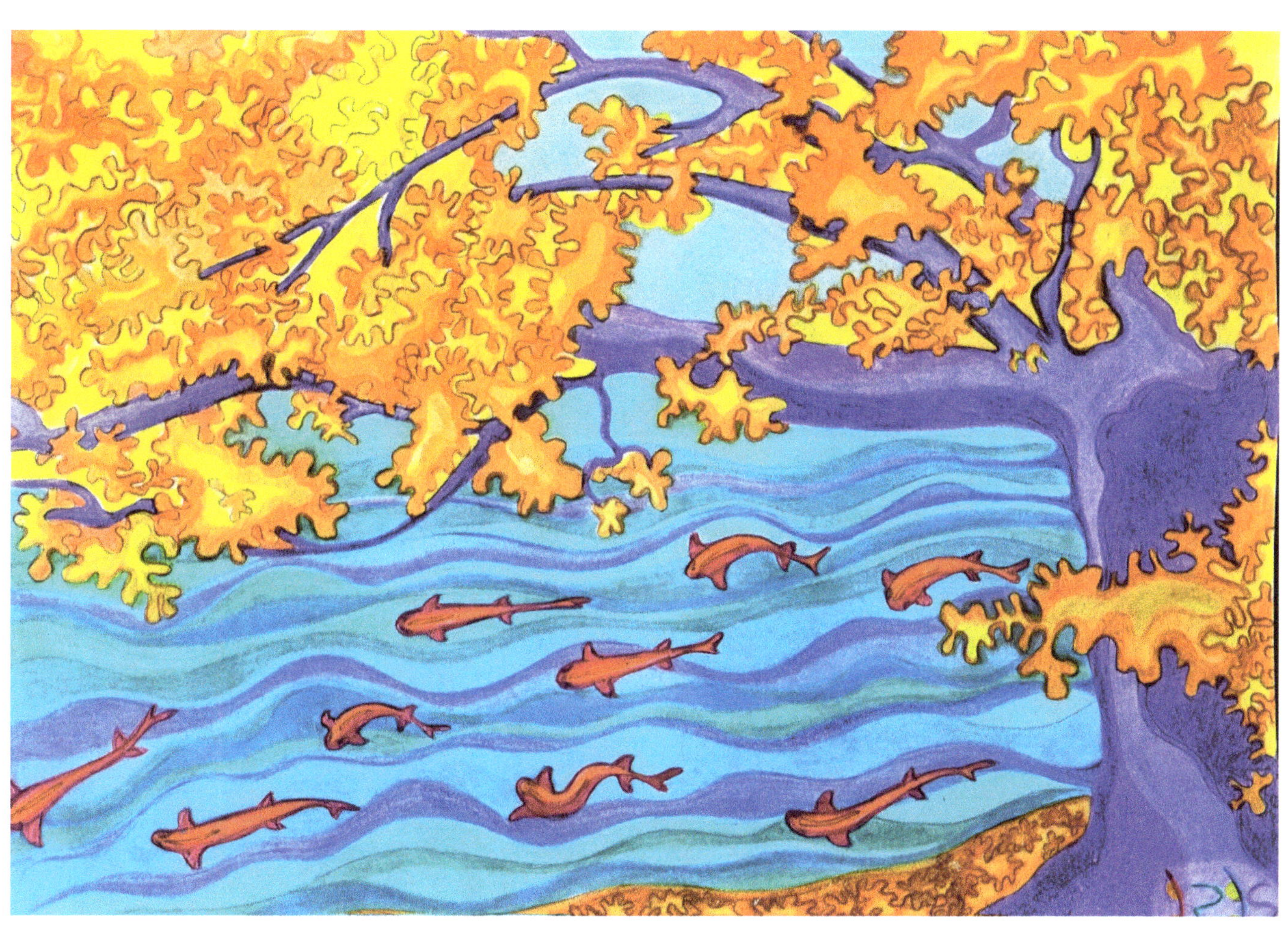

Landscape with Sycamore Tree and Goldfish. Color pencils. 30x21cm. 2024

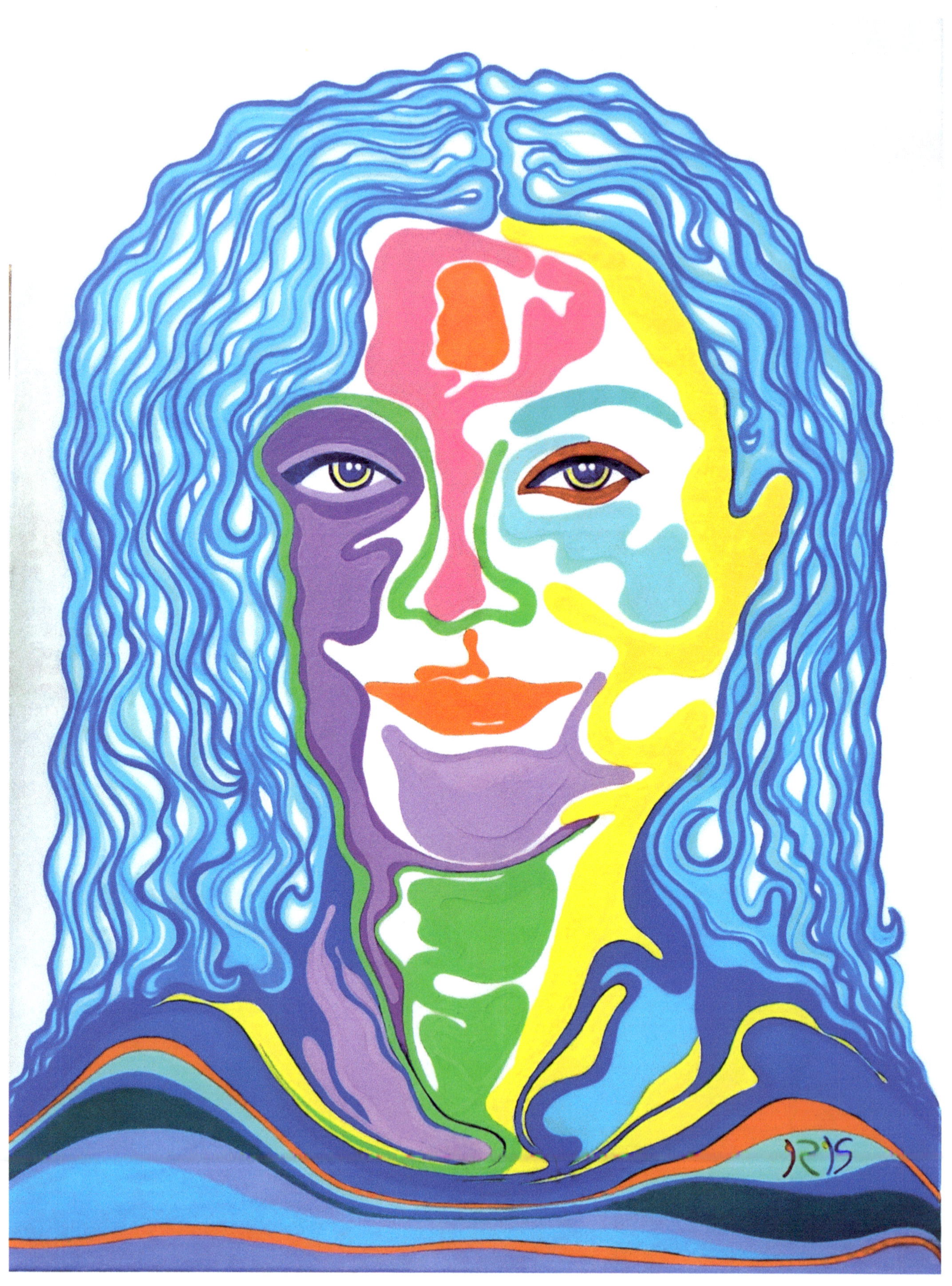

Self-portrait. Acrylic. 70x50cm. 2024

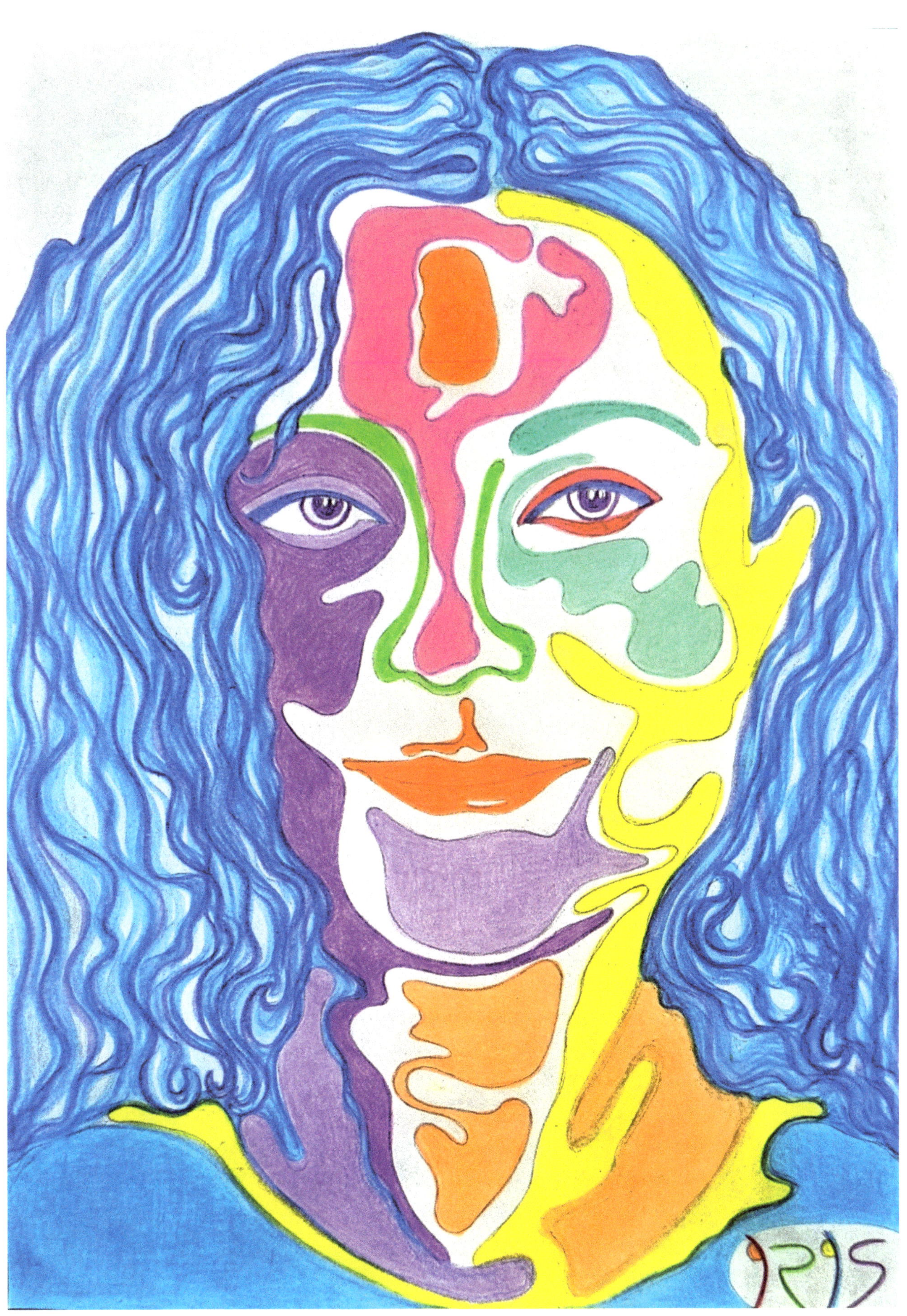

Self-portrait. color pencils. 30x21cm. 2024

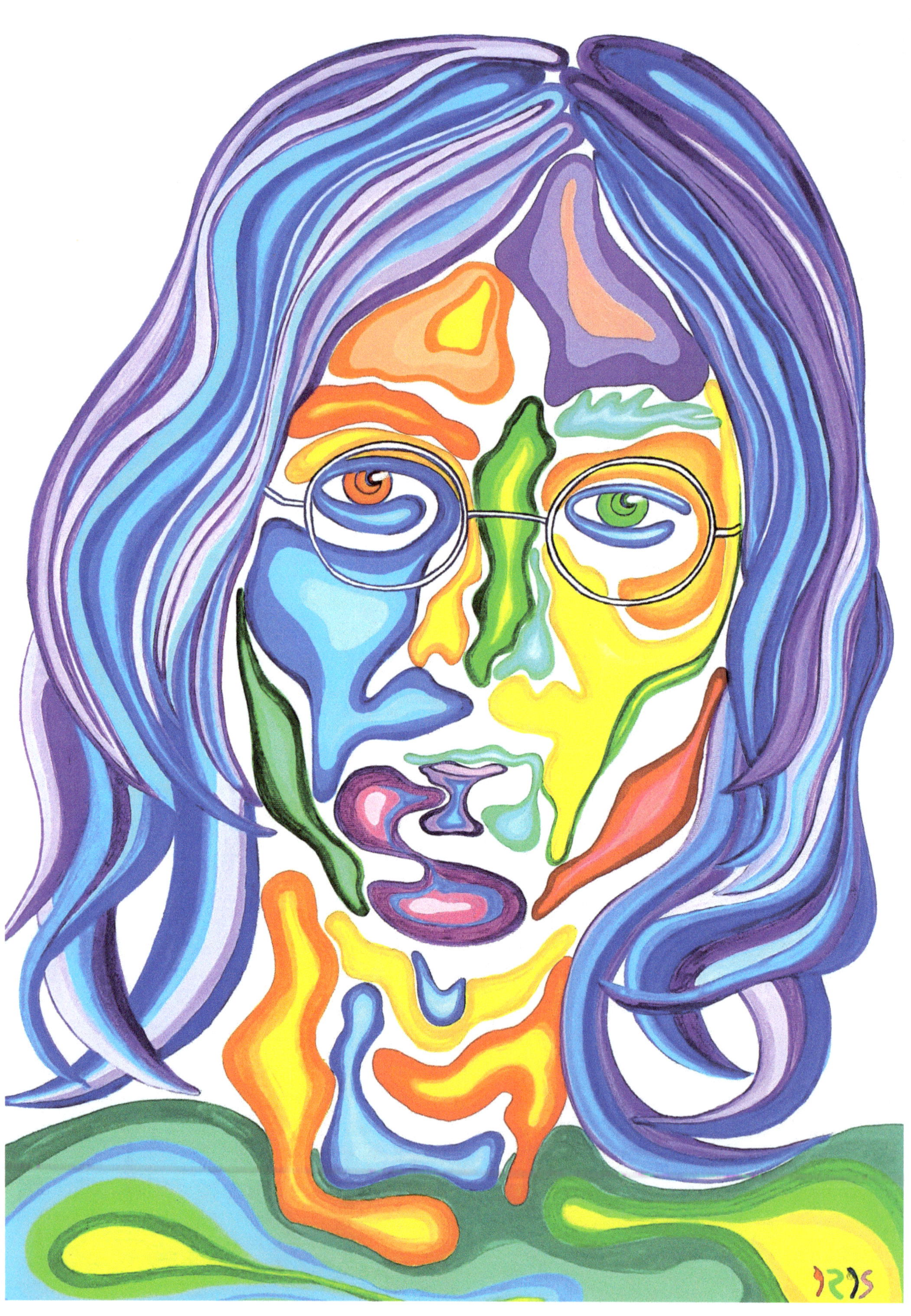

John Lennon. Acrylic. 80x60cm. 2021

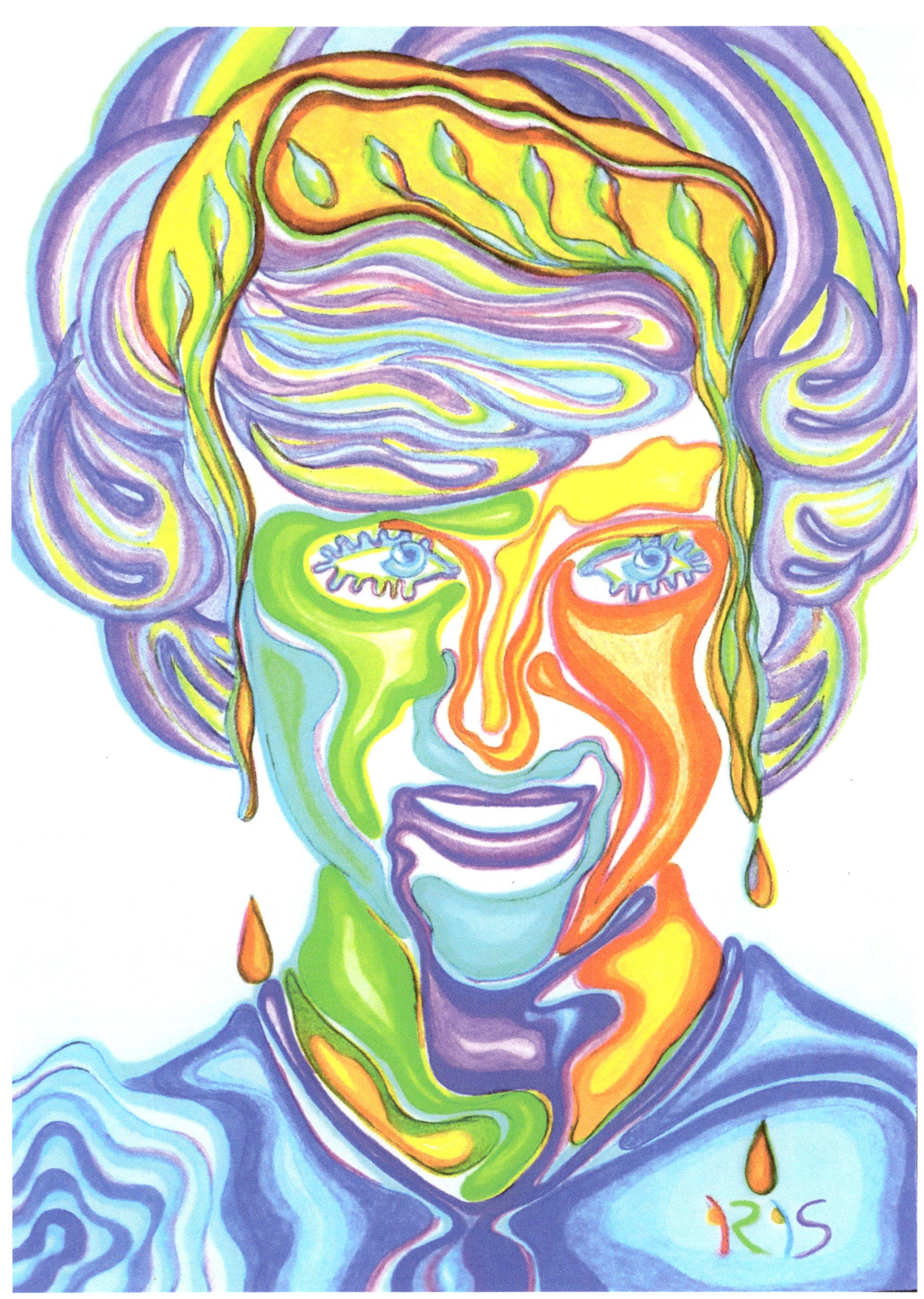

Lady Diana.Color pencils.30x21cm.2022

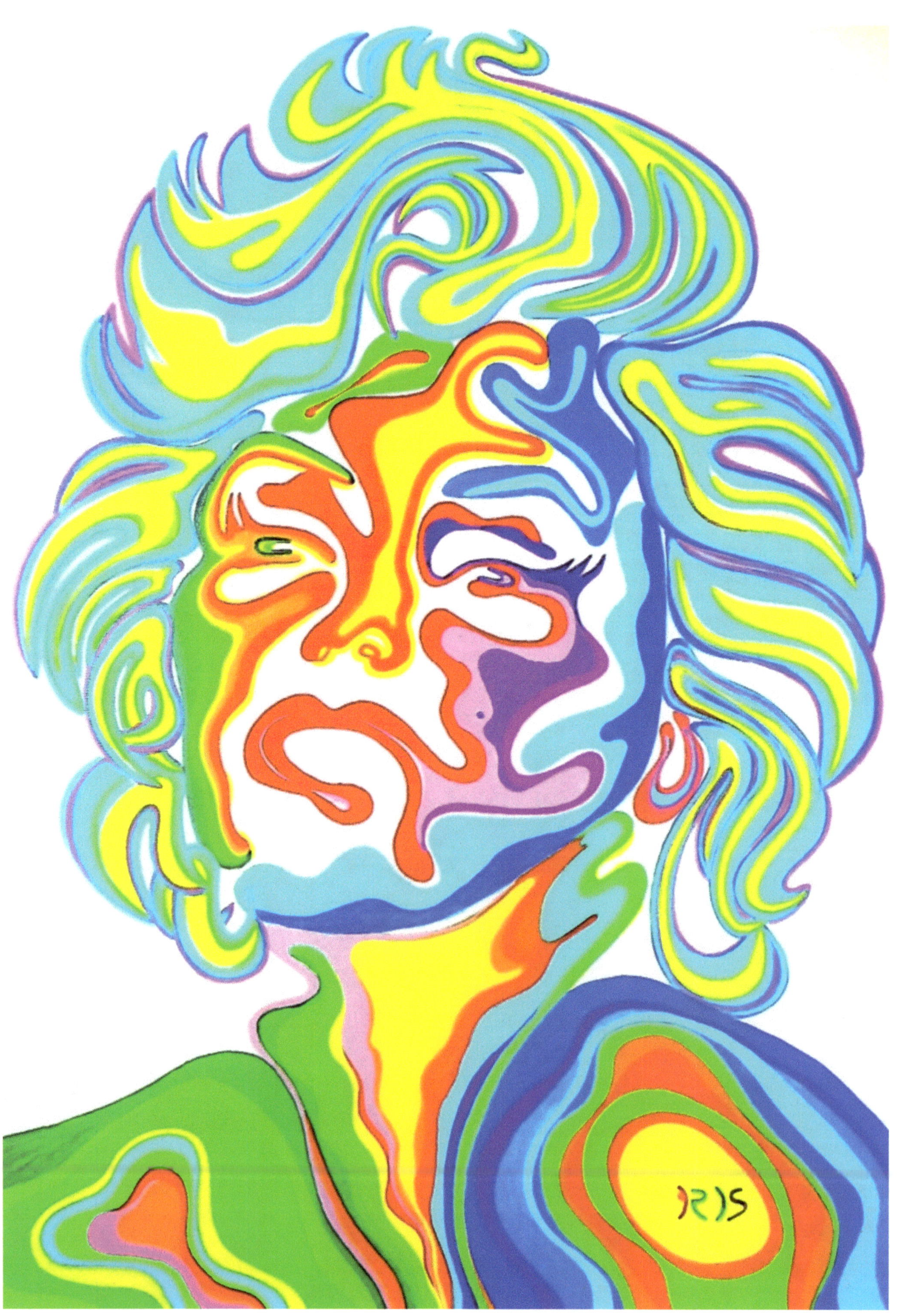

Marilyn Monroe. Acrylic.80x60cm.2021

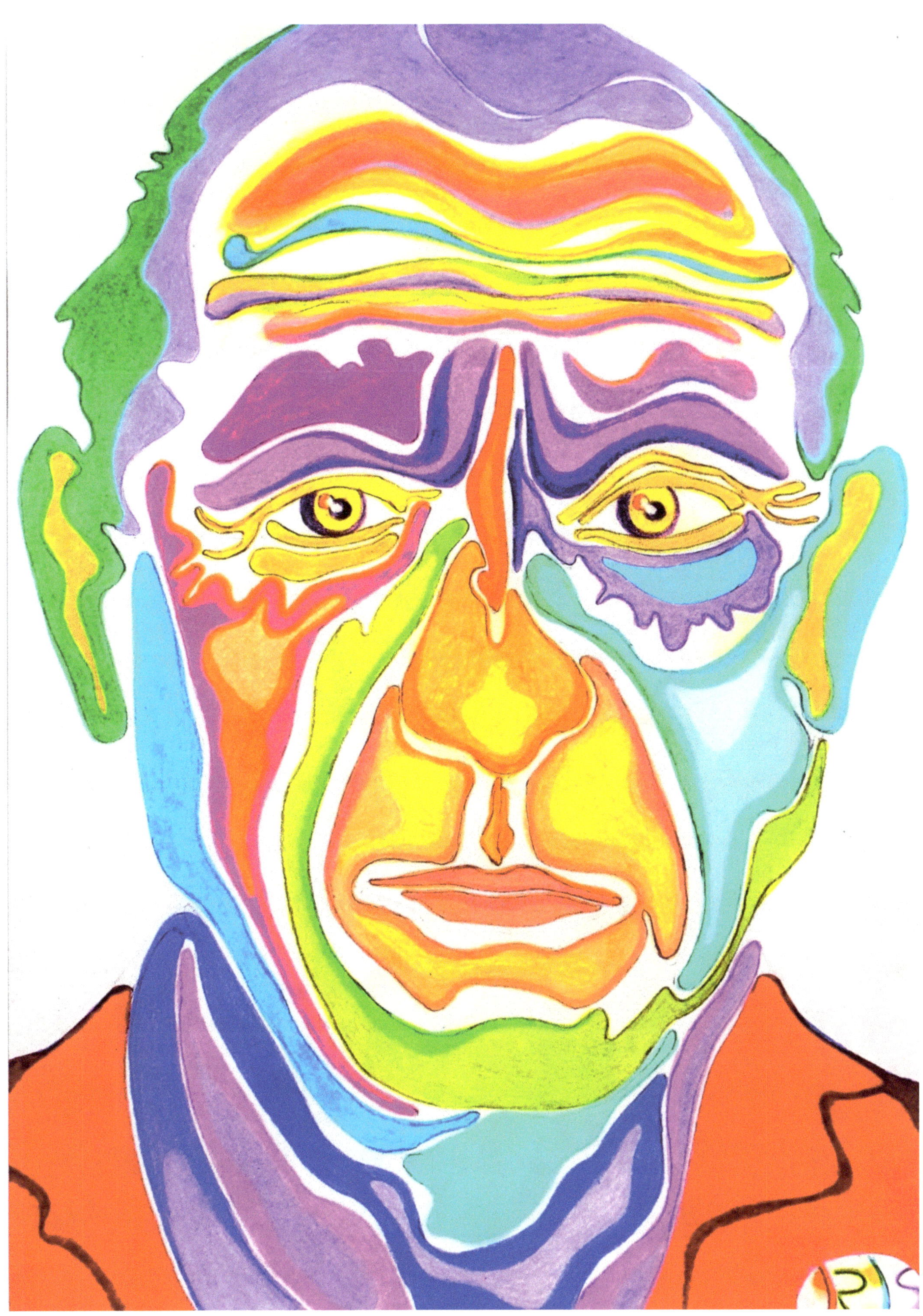

Pablo Picasso. Color pencils.30x21cm.2023

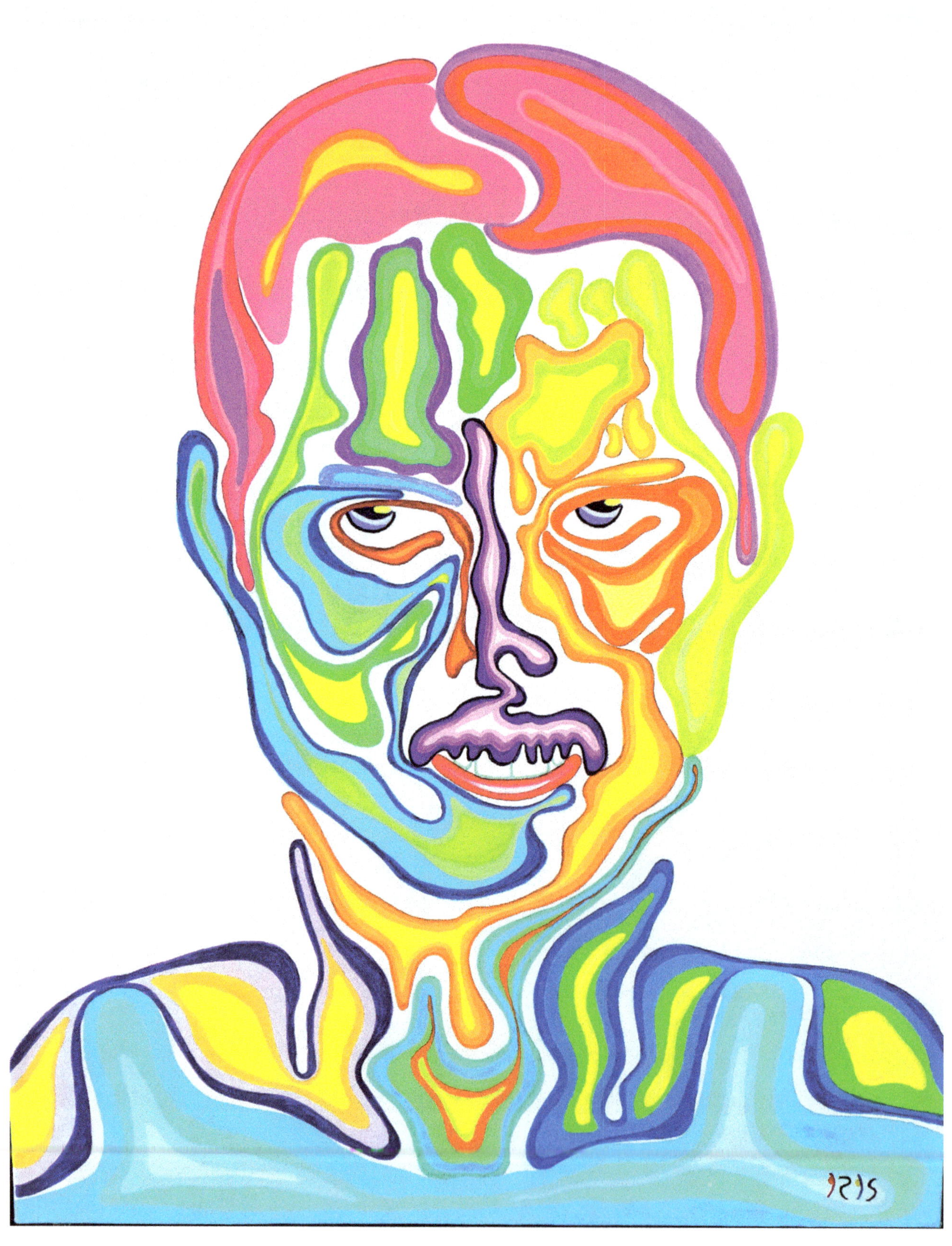

Freddie Mercury. Acrylic. 80x60cm. 2021

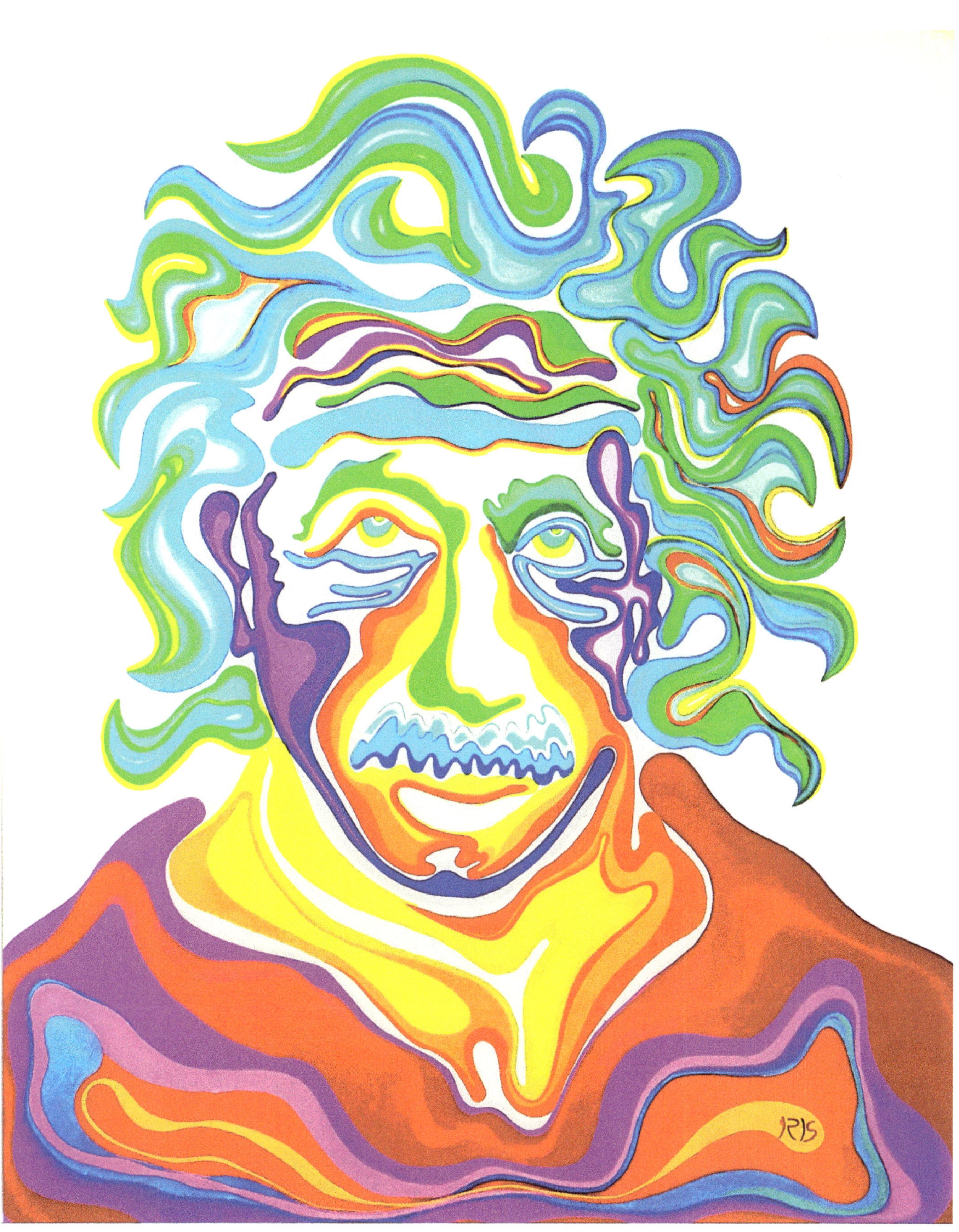

Albert Einstein. Acrylic.100x80cm.2021

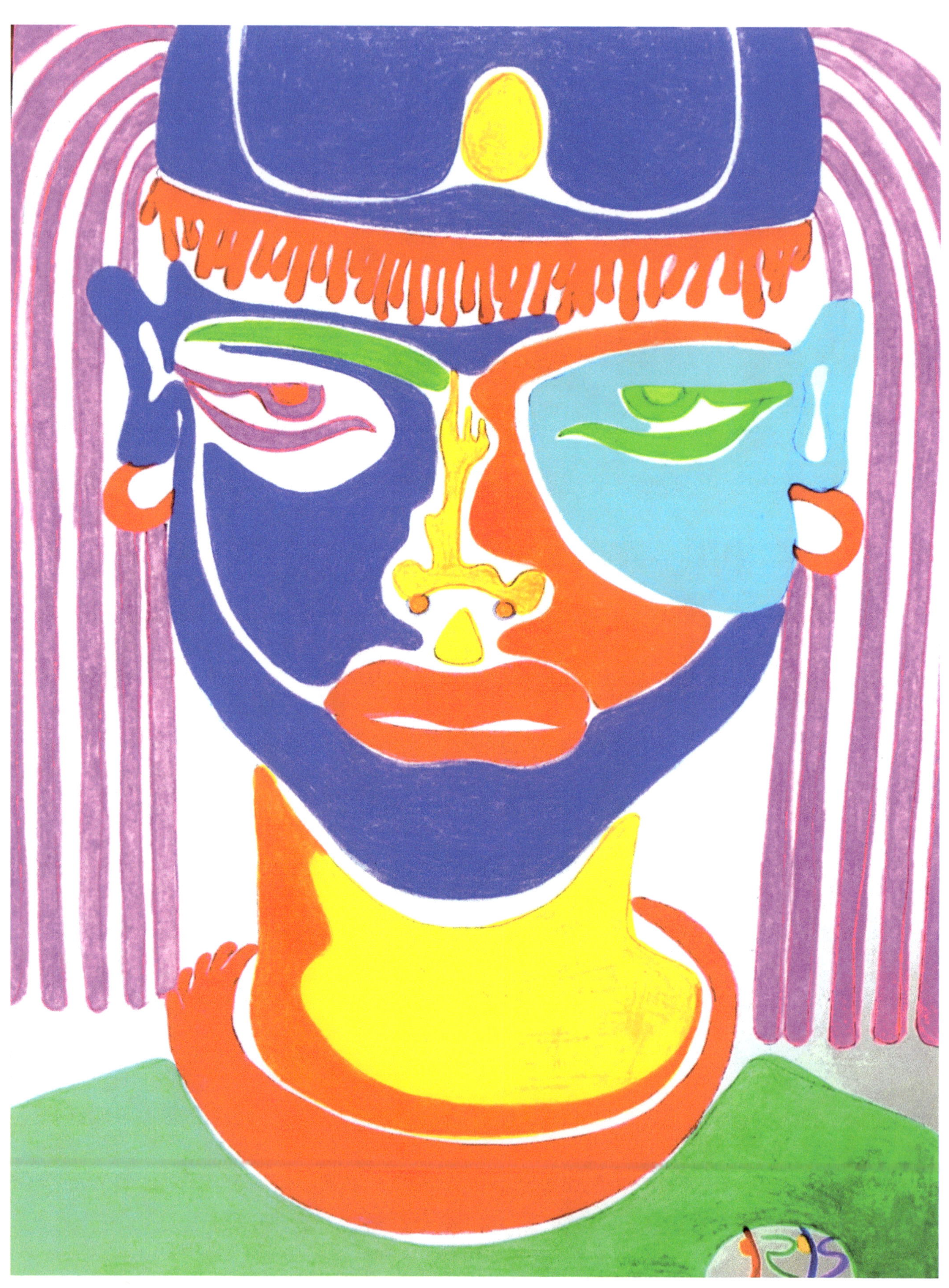

African Princess. Color pencils. 30x21cm.2023

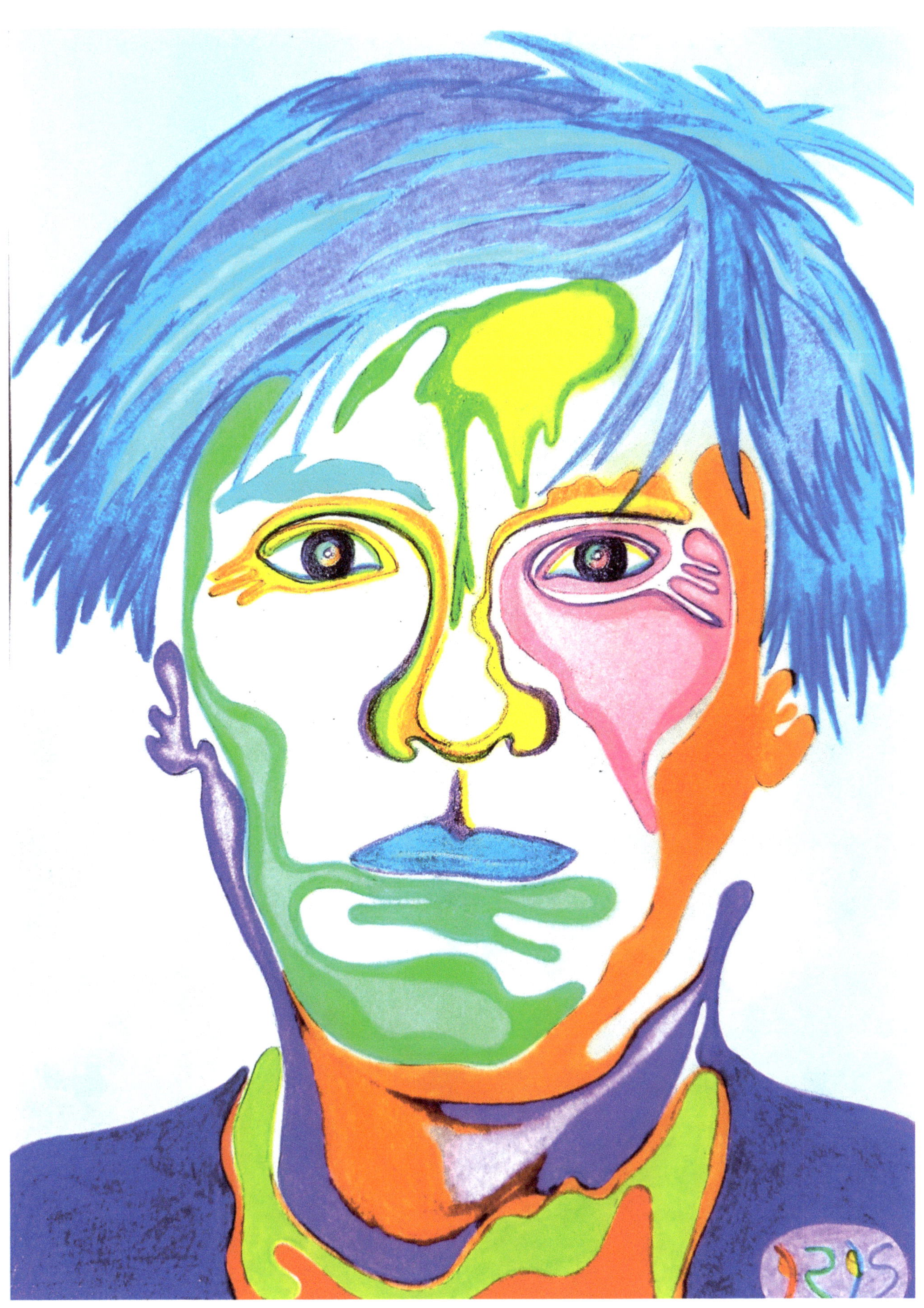

Andy Warhol.Color pencils.30x21cm.2024

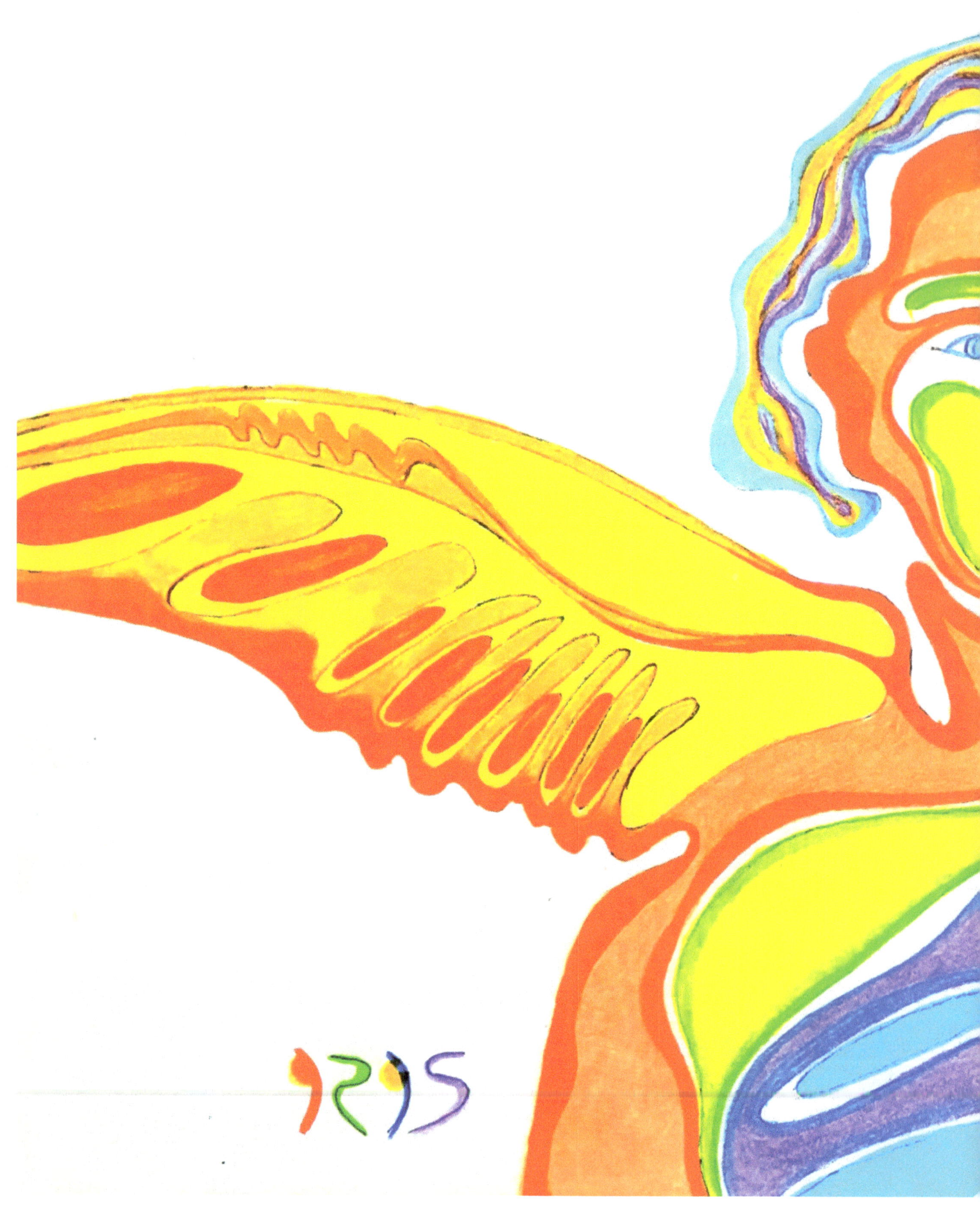

Angel of Pace and Joy.Color pencils.30x21cm.2022

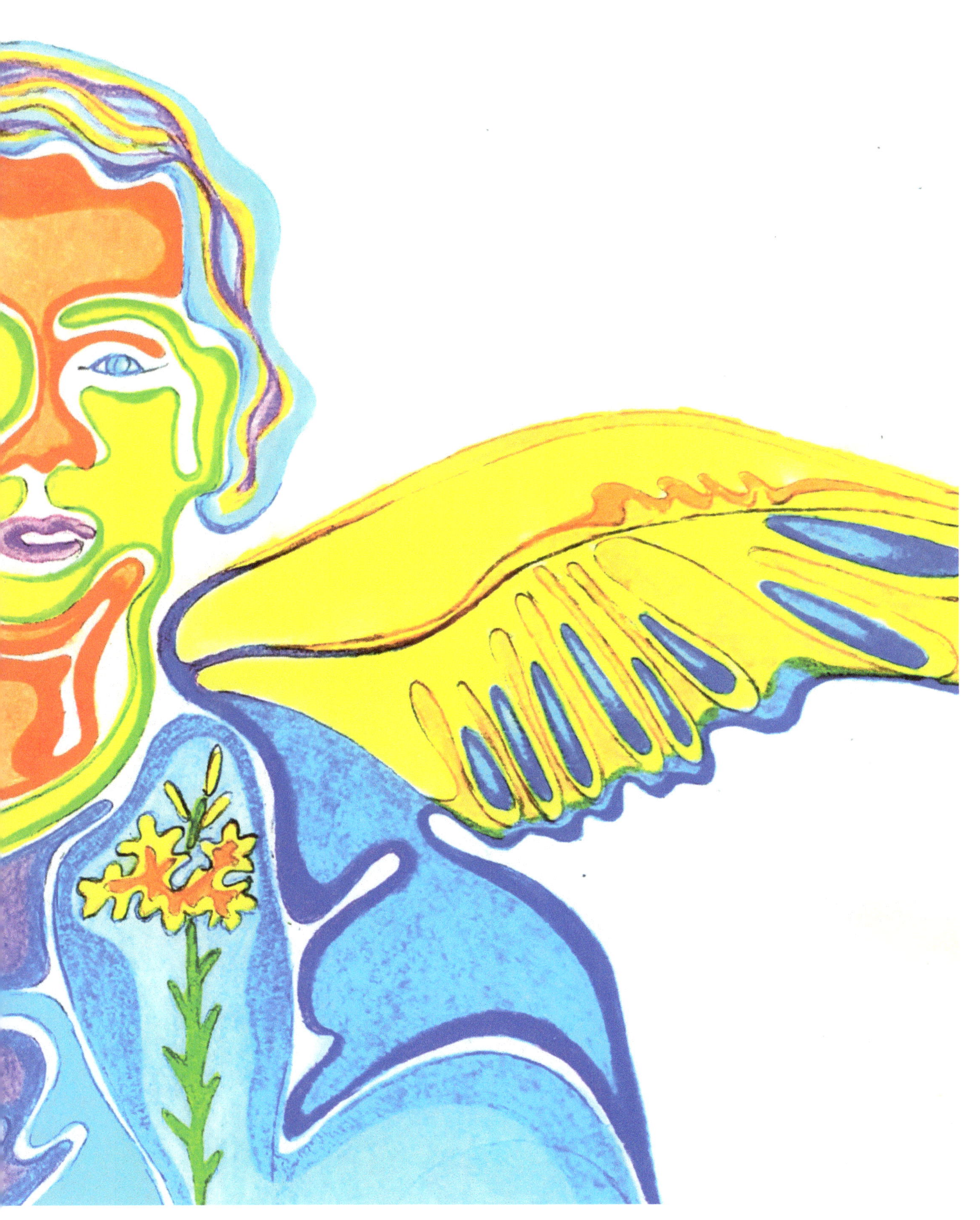

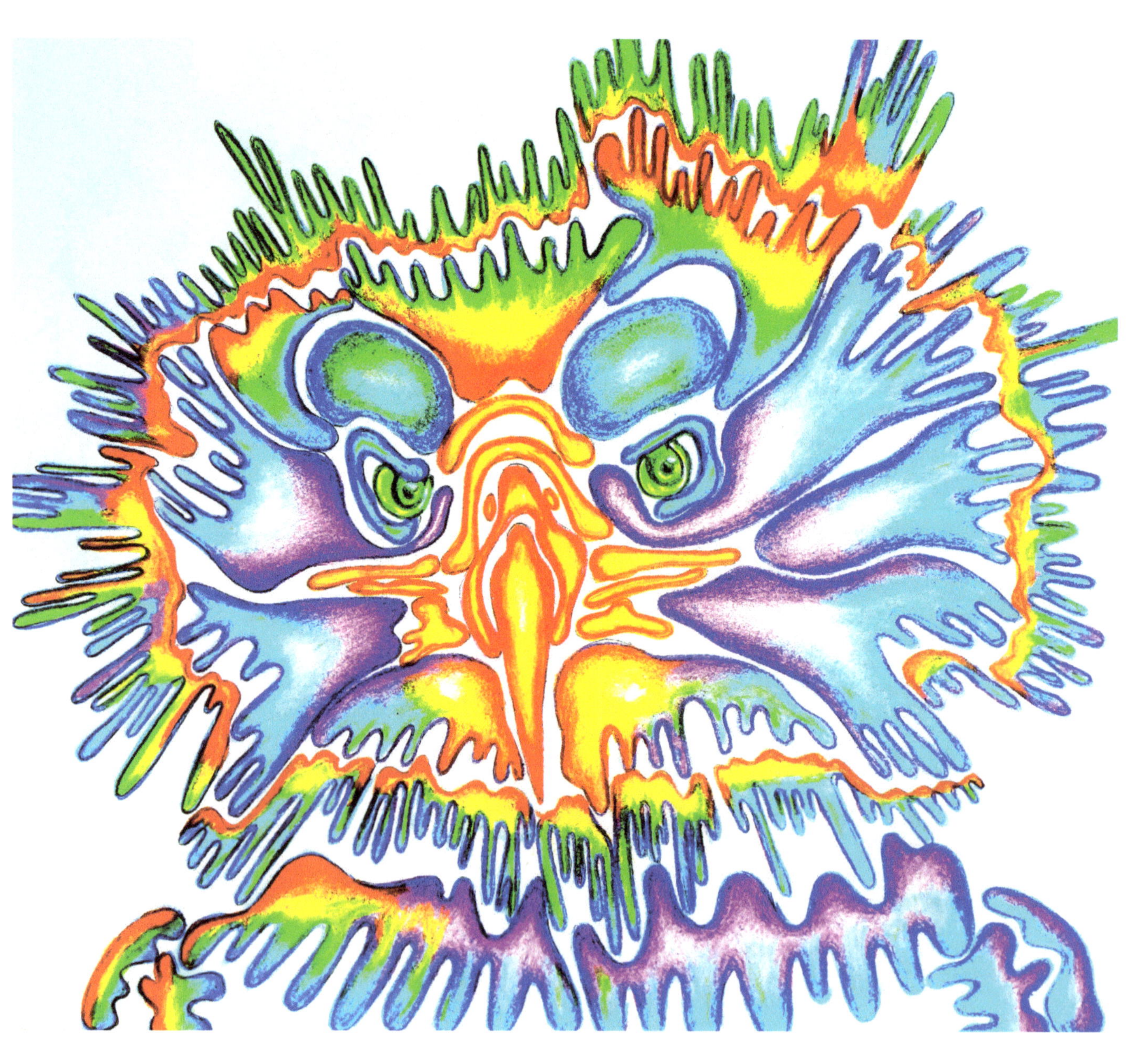

Angry Eagle.Color pencils.30x21cm.2019

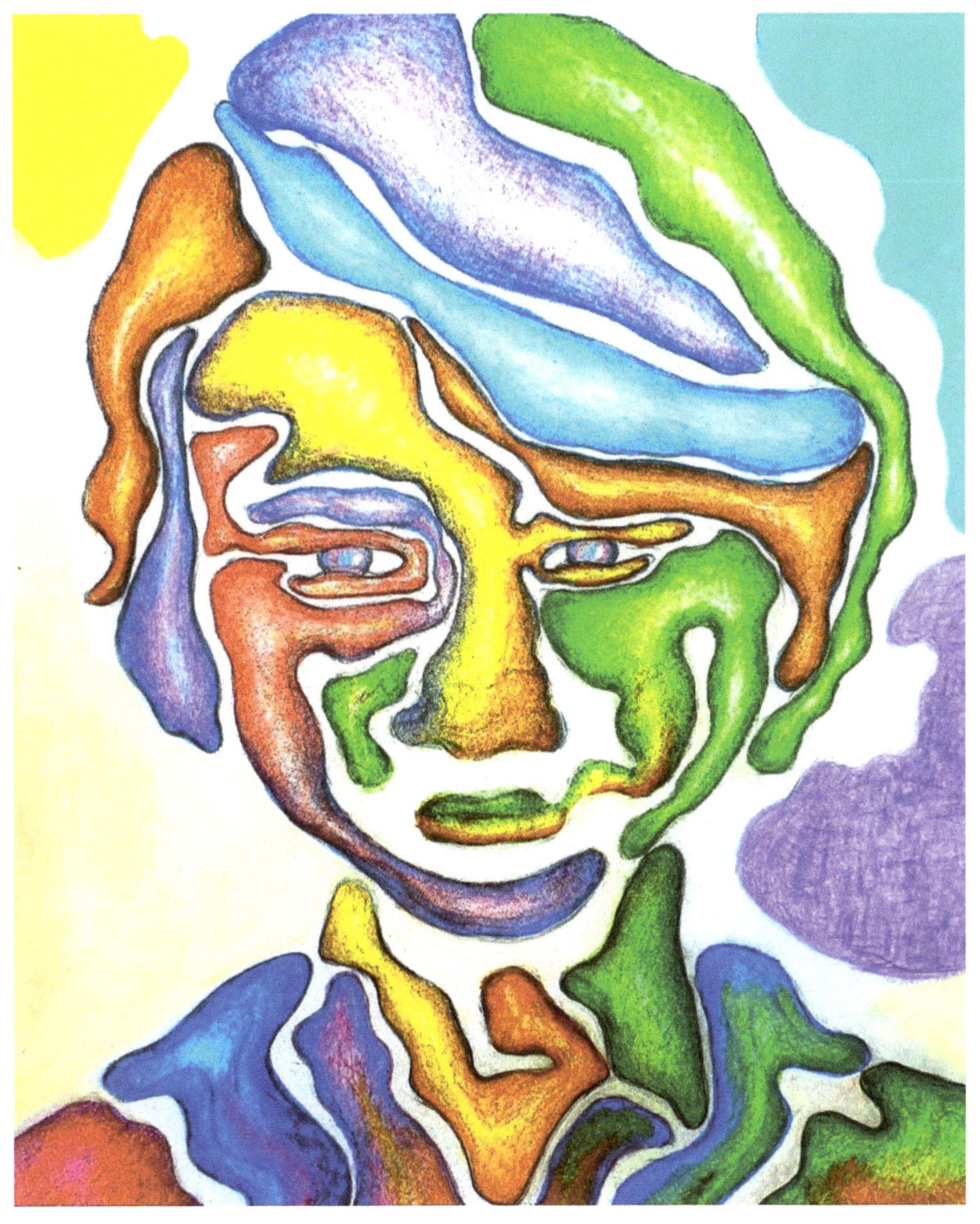

Arthur.Color Pencils.30x21cm.2019

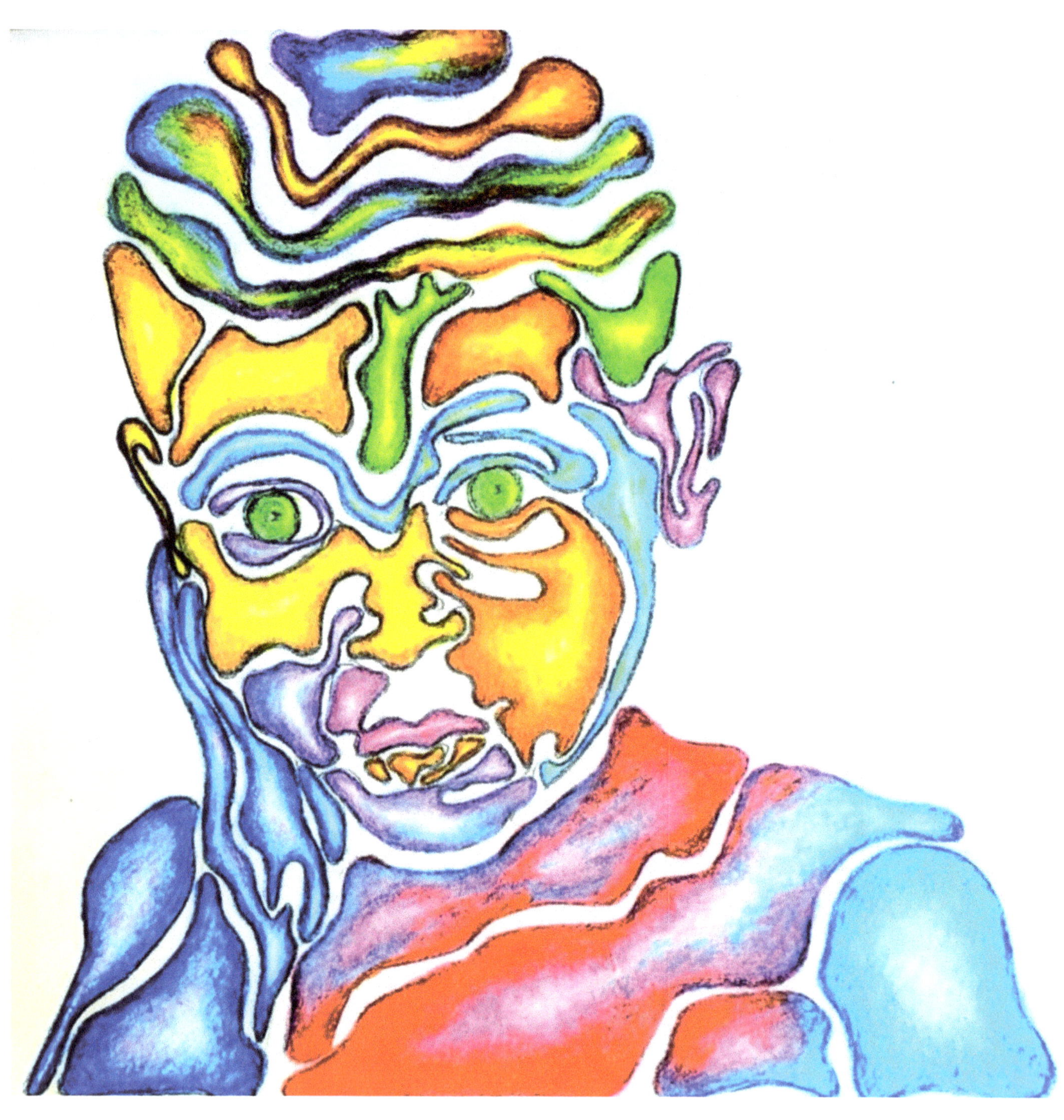

Boy with green eyes.Color pencils.30x21cm.2019

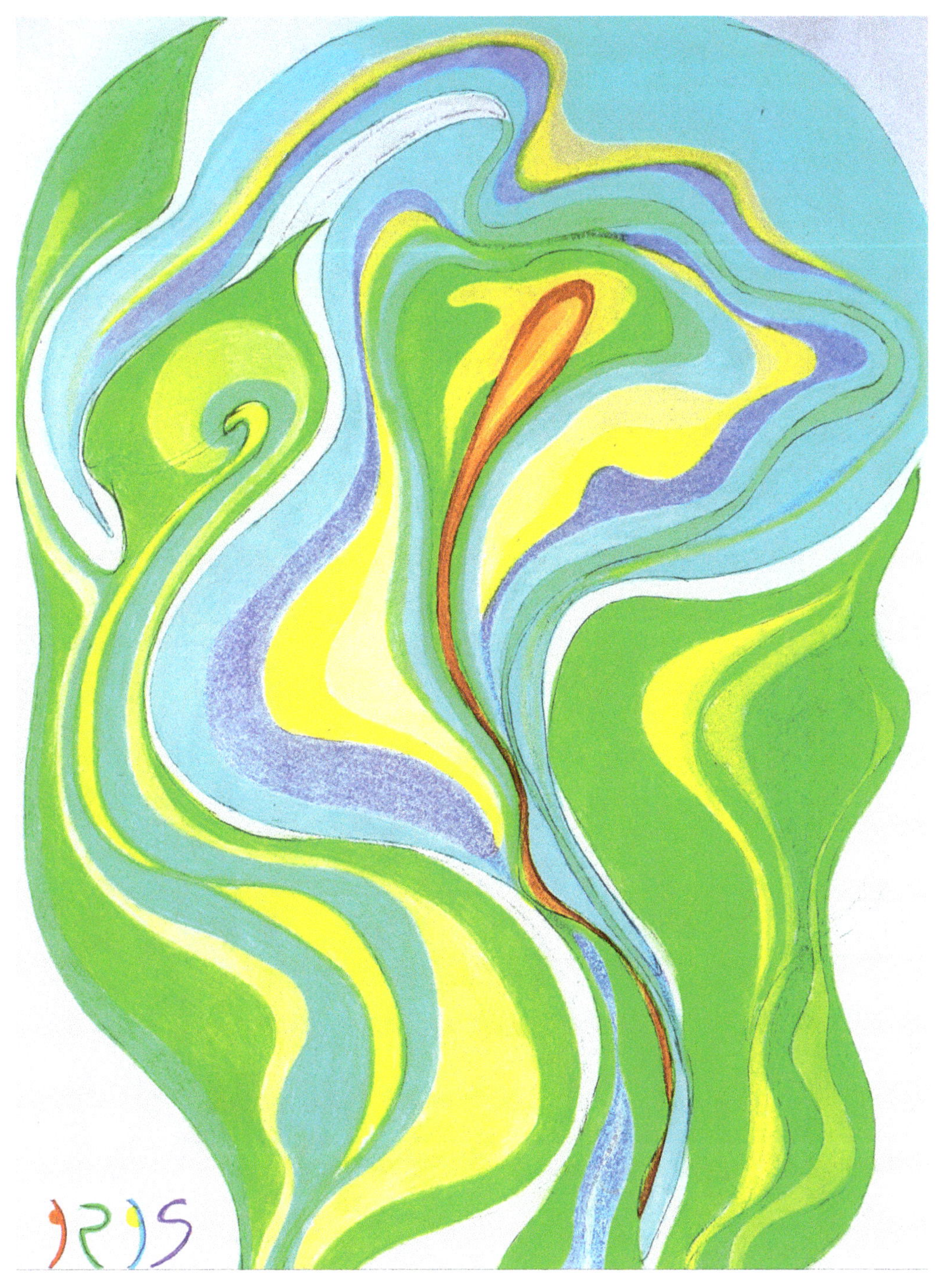

Calla lily. Color pencils. 30x21cm. 2021

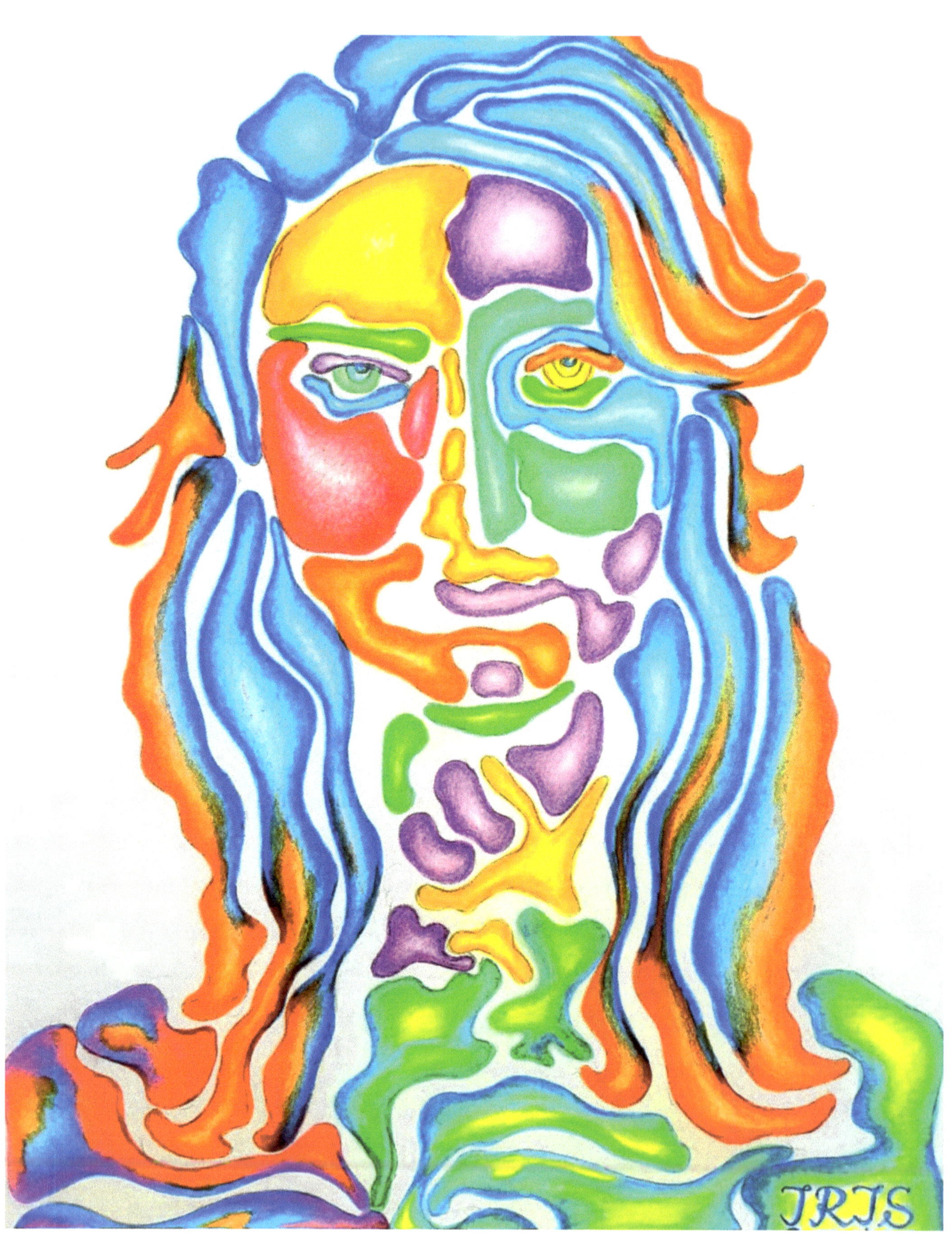

Claire. Color pencils.30x21cm.2019

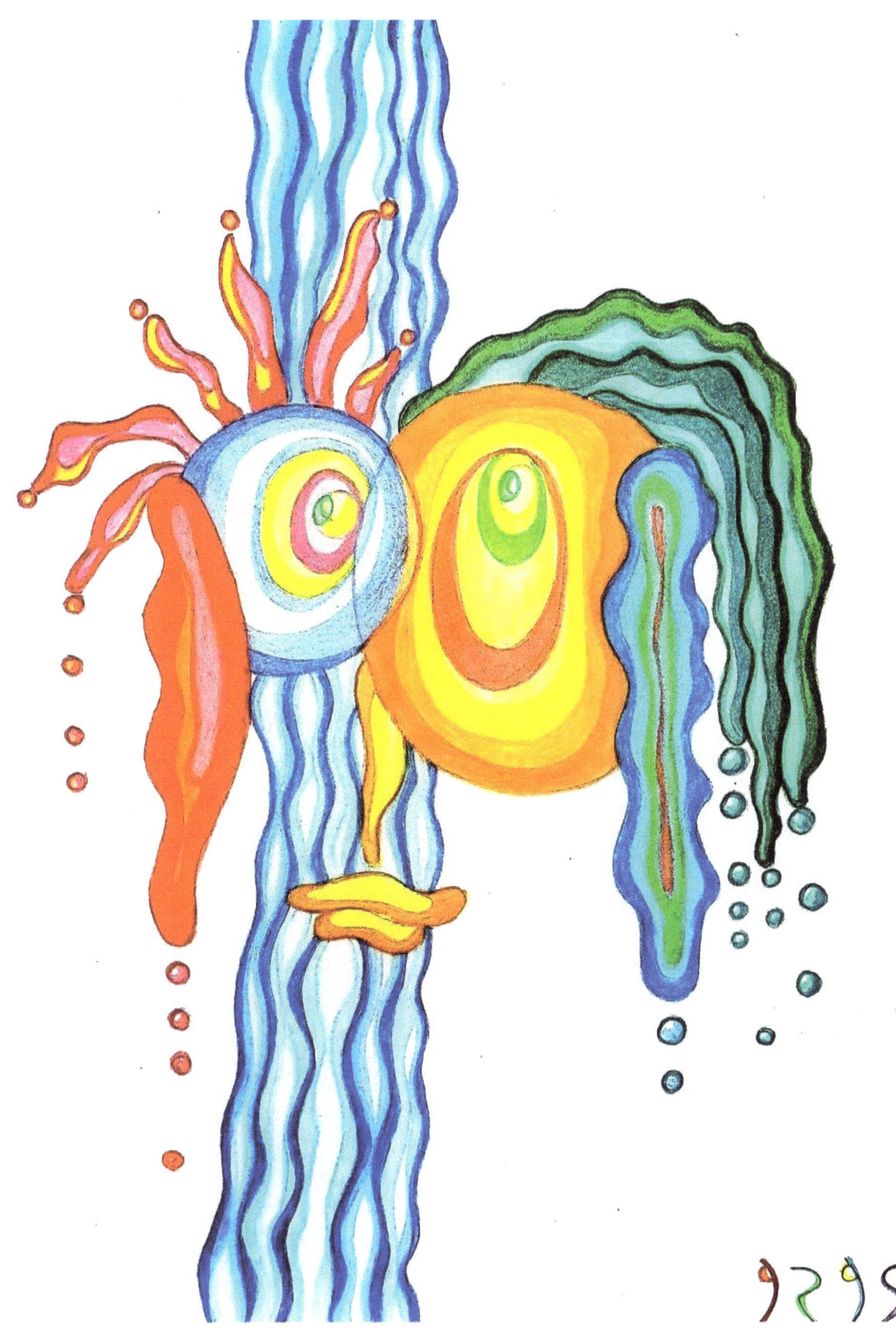

Dolly duck.Color pencils.30x21cm.2021

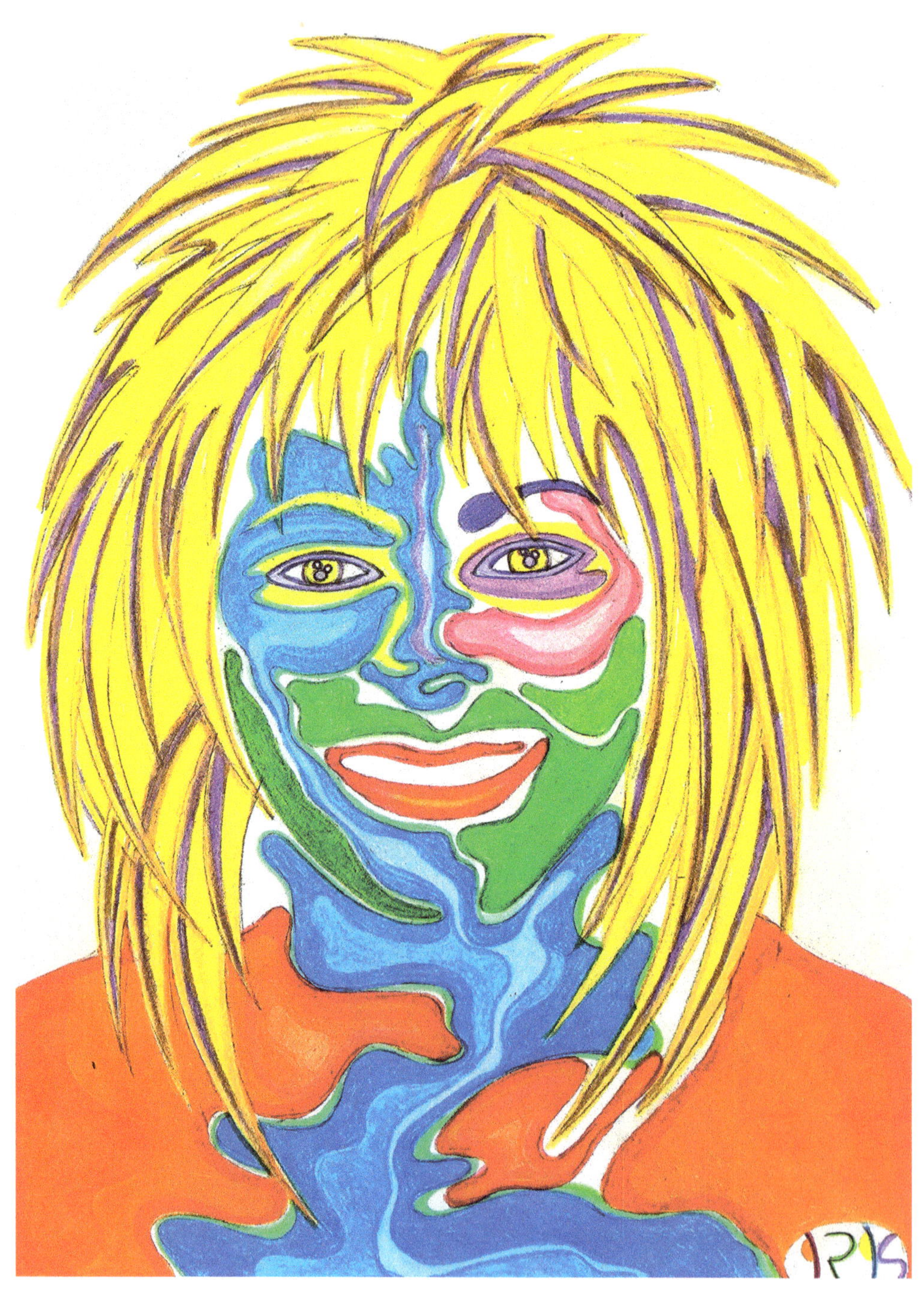

Tina Turner. Color pencils. 30x21cm.2023

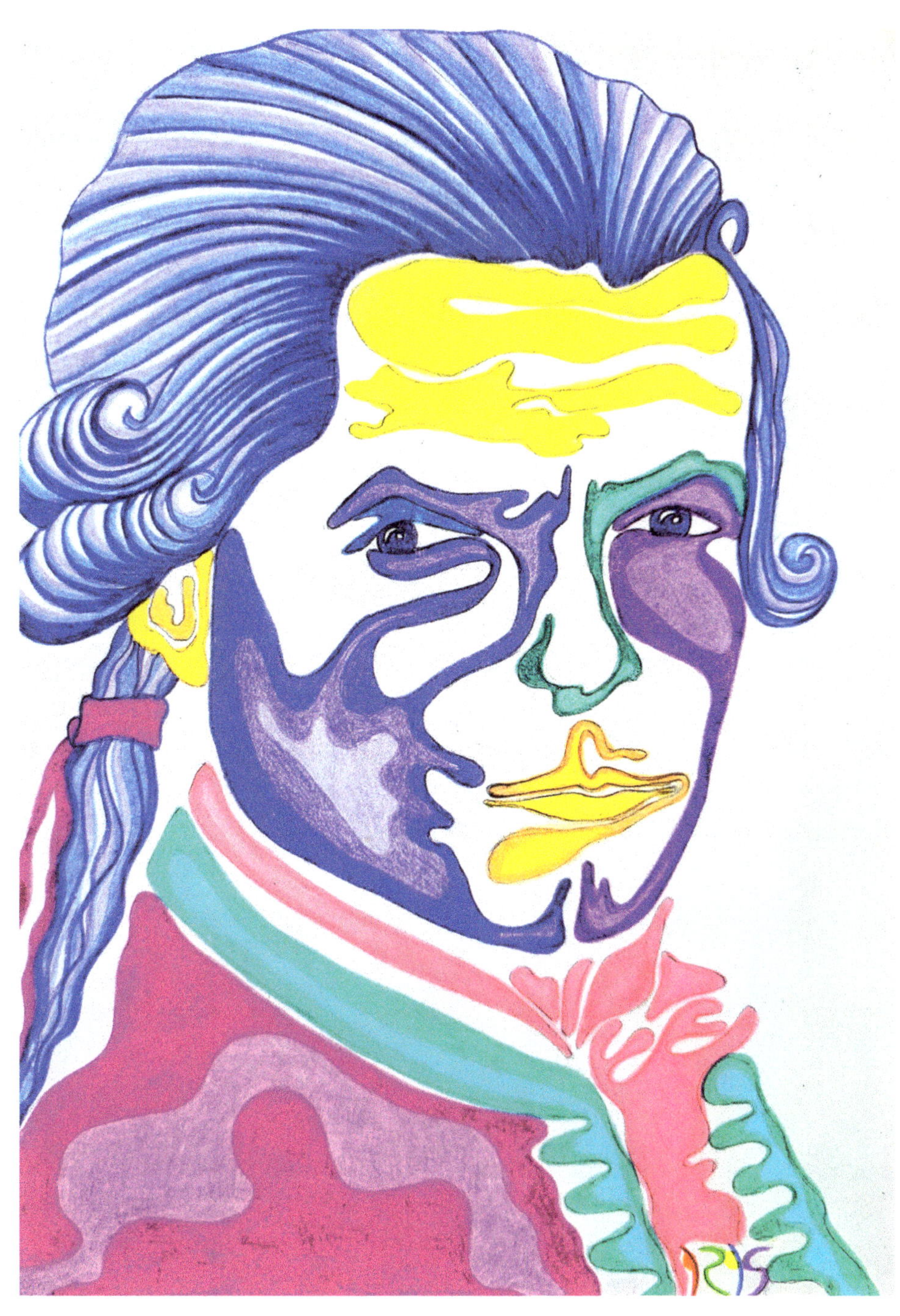

Falco_Amadeus Mozart.Color pencils.30x21cm.2023

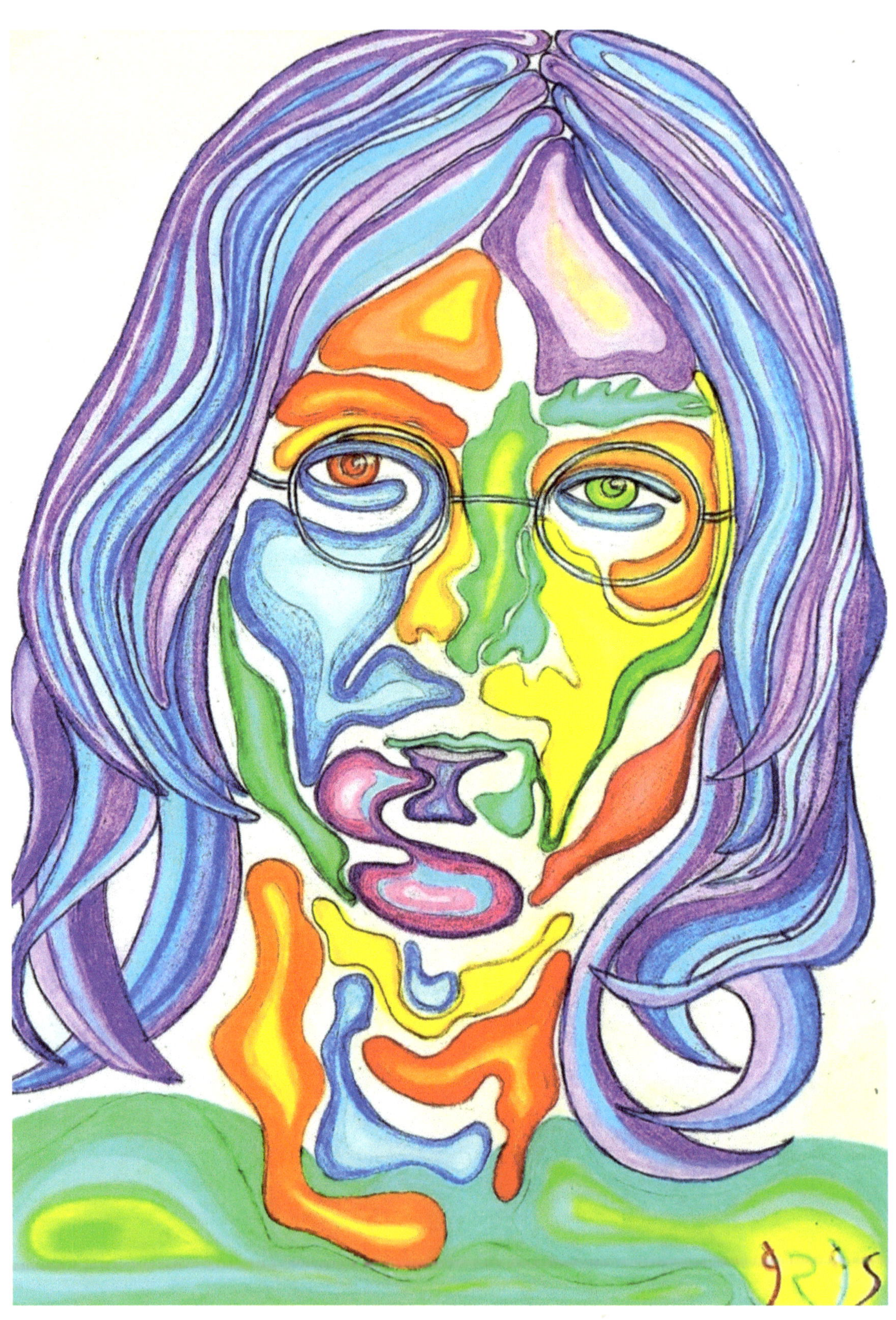

John Lennon. Color pencils. 30x21cm. 2020

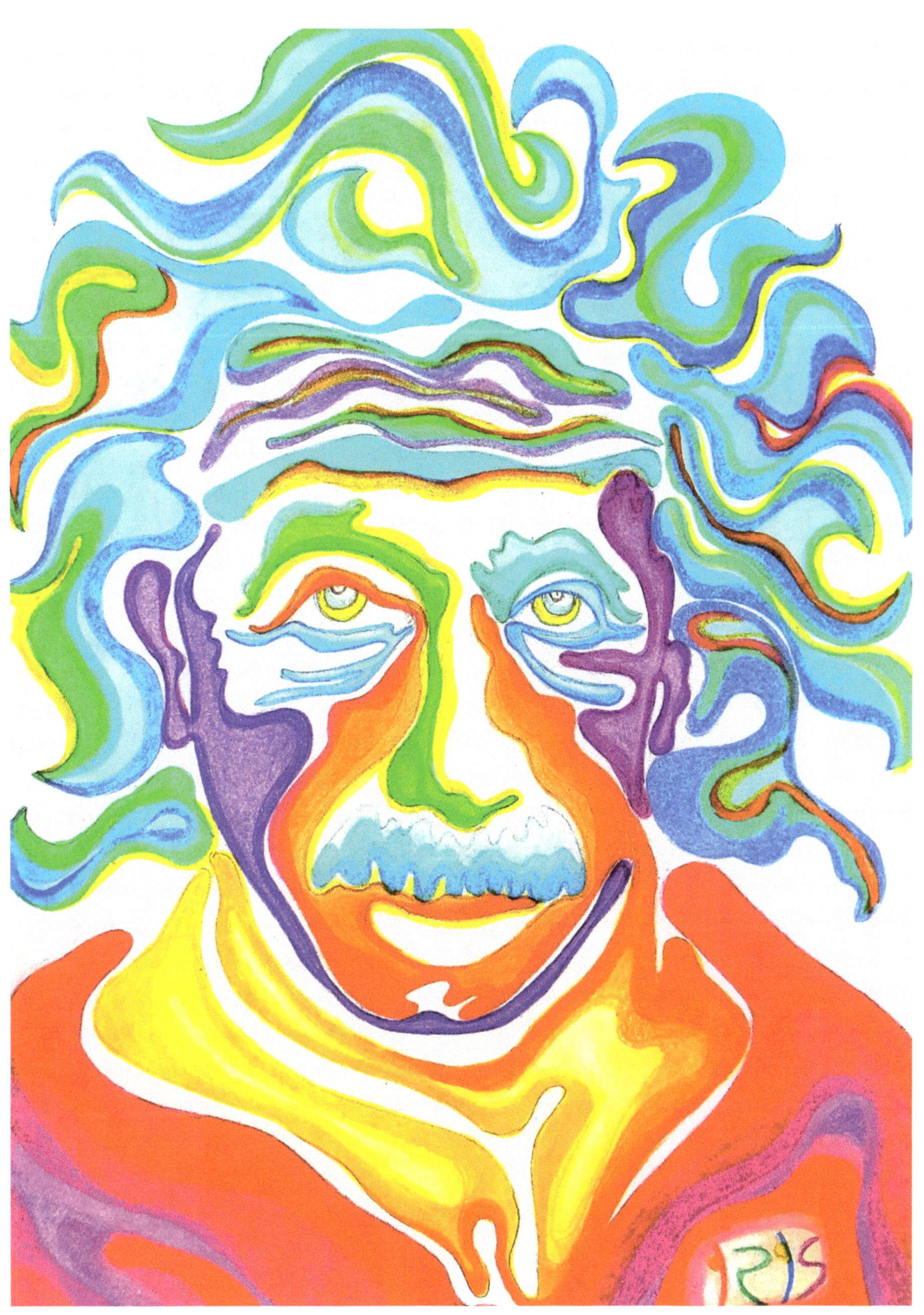

Albert Einstein. Color pencils. 30x21cm. 2021

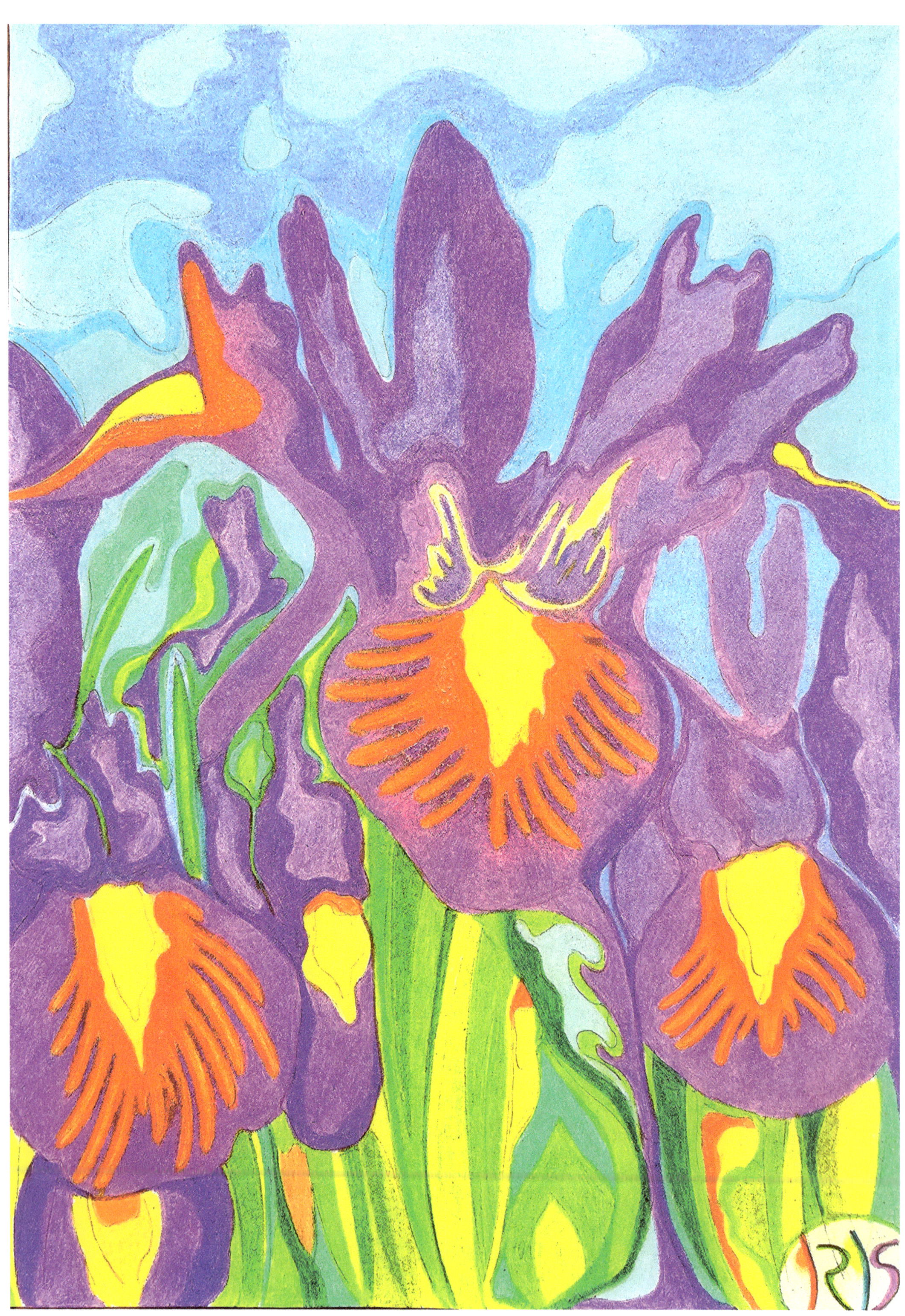

Flowers.Color pencils.30x21cm.2023

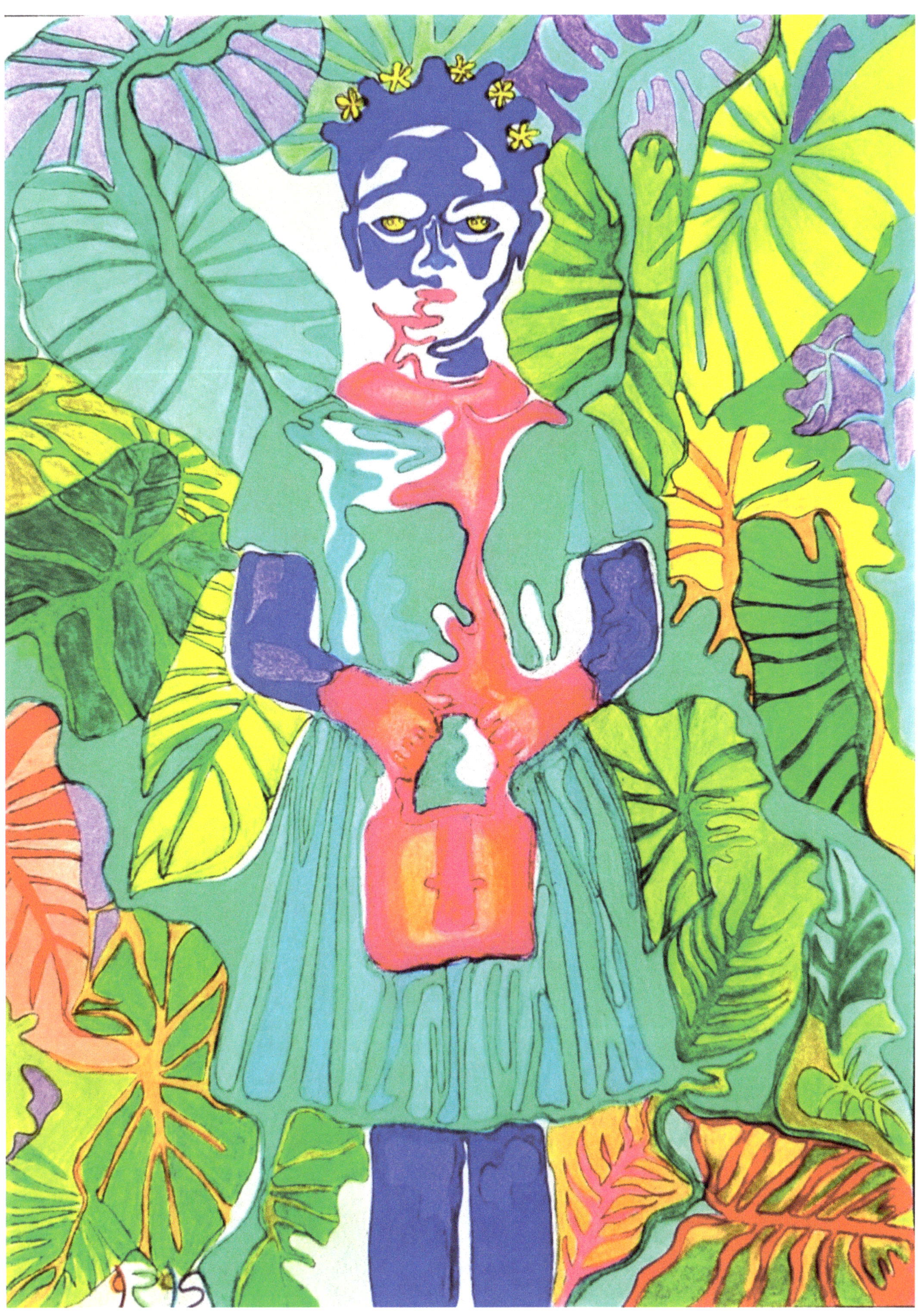

Fluid connections. Color pencils.30x21cm. 2023

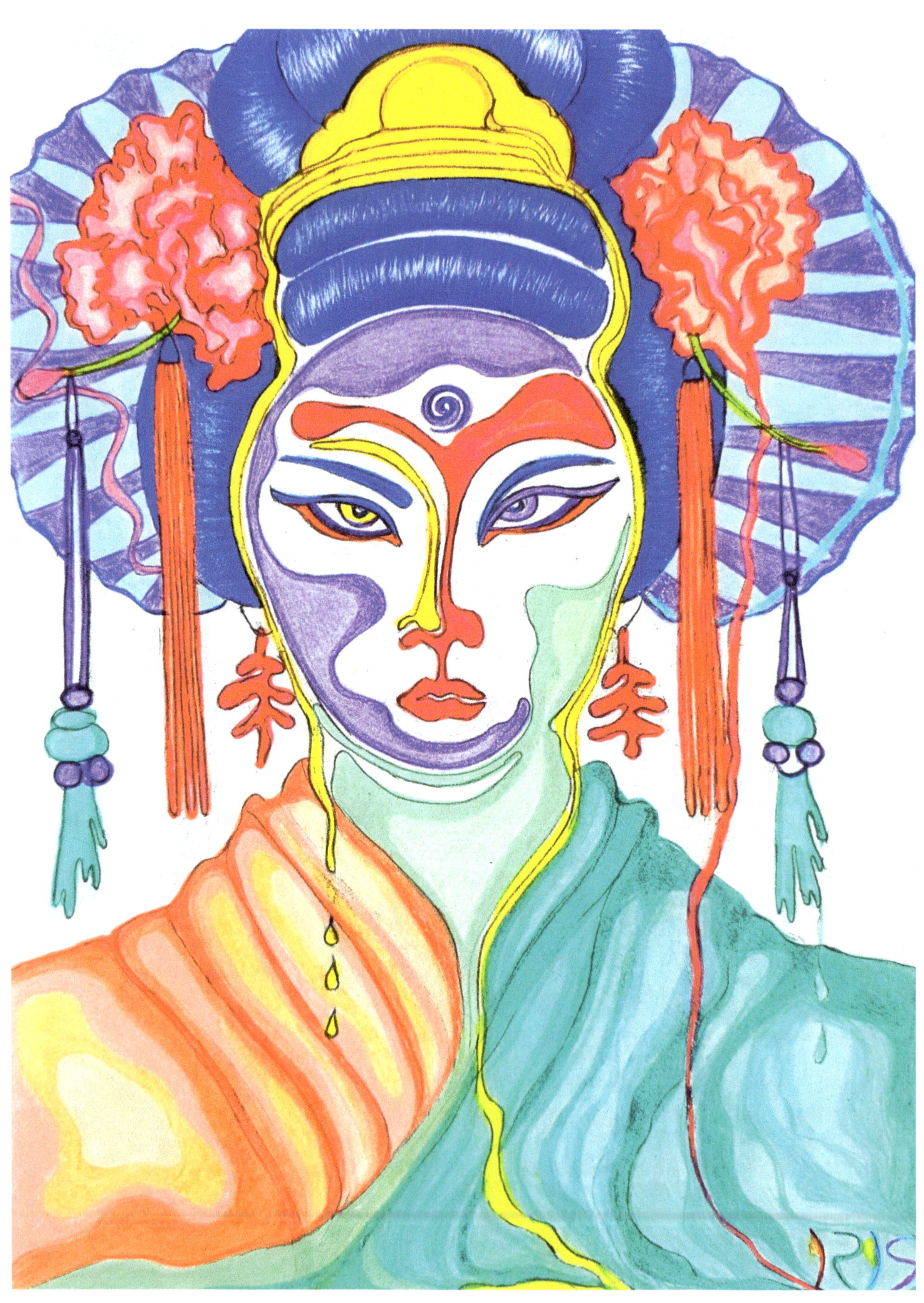

Geisha.Color pencils.30x21cm. 2024

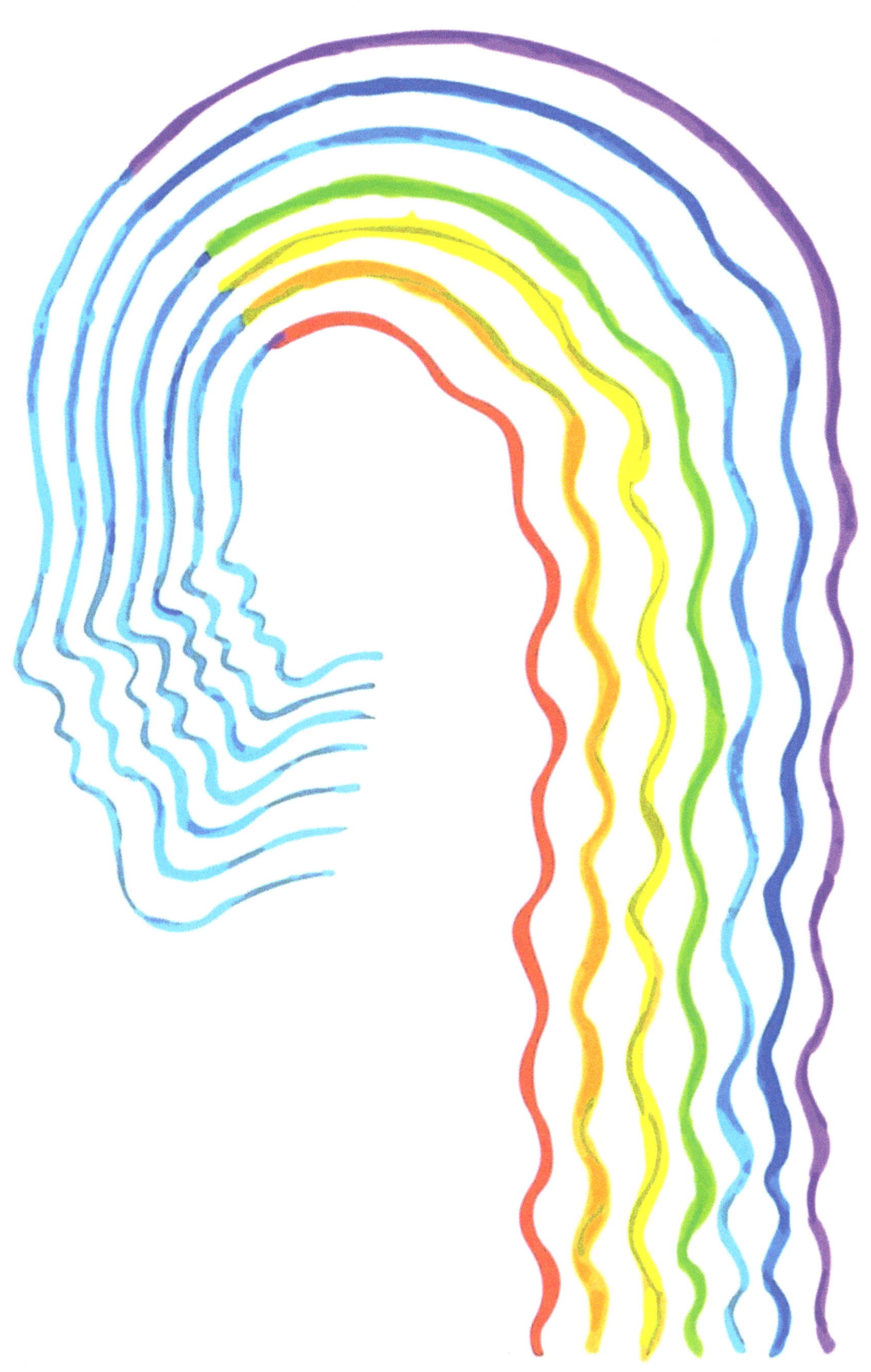

IRIS_FLUIDISM_logo.Color pencils.30x21cm.2022

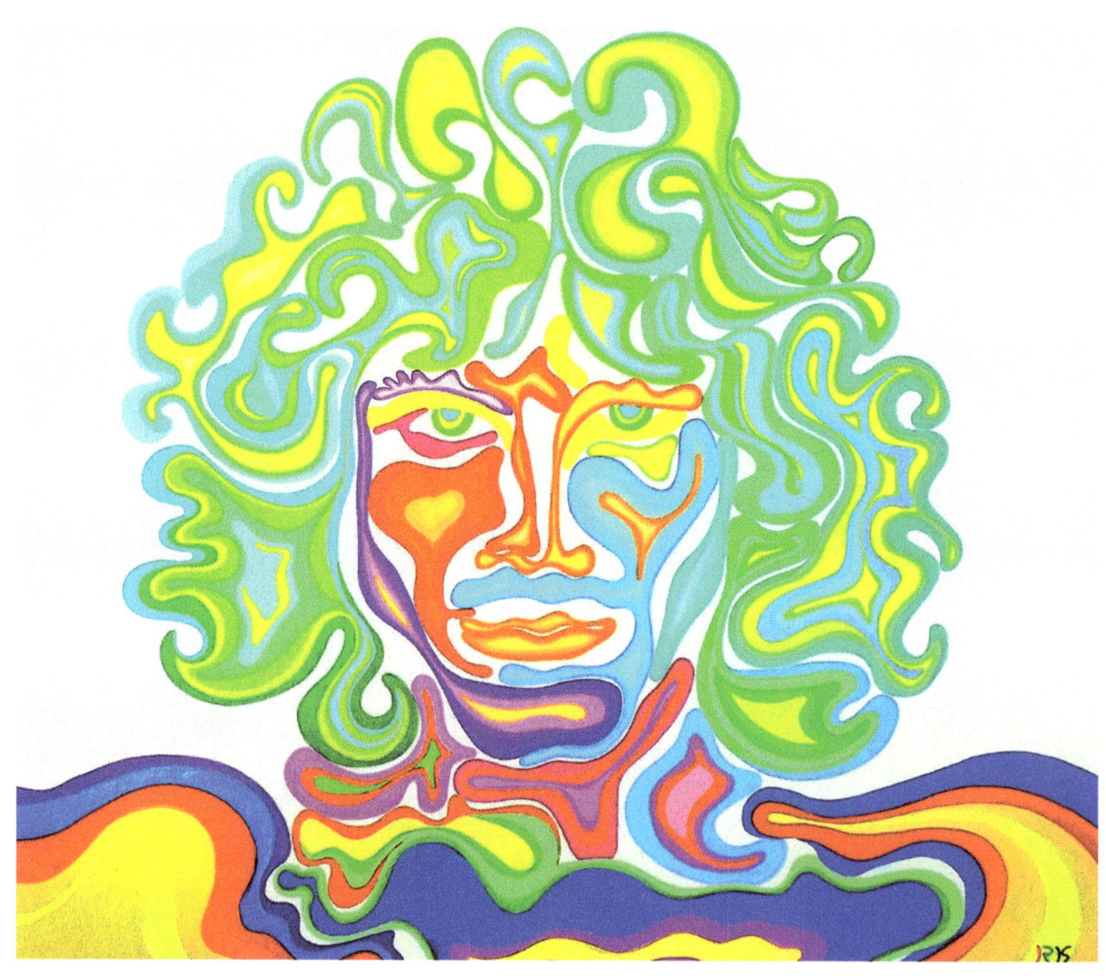

Jim Morrison. Acrylic.100x80cm.2022

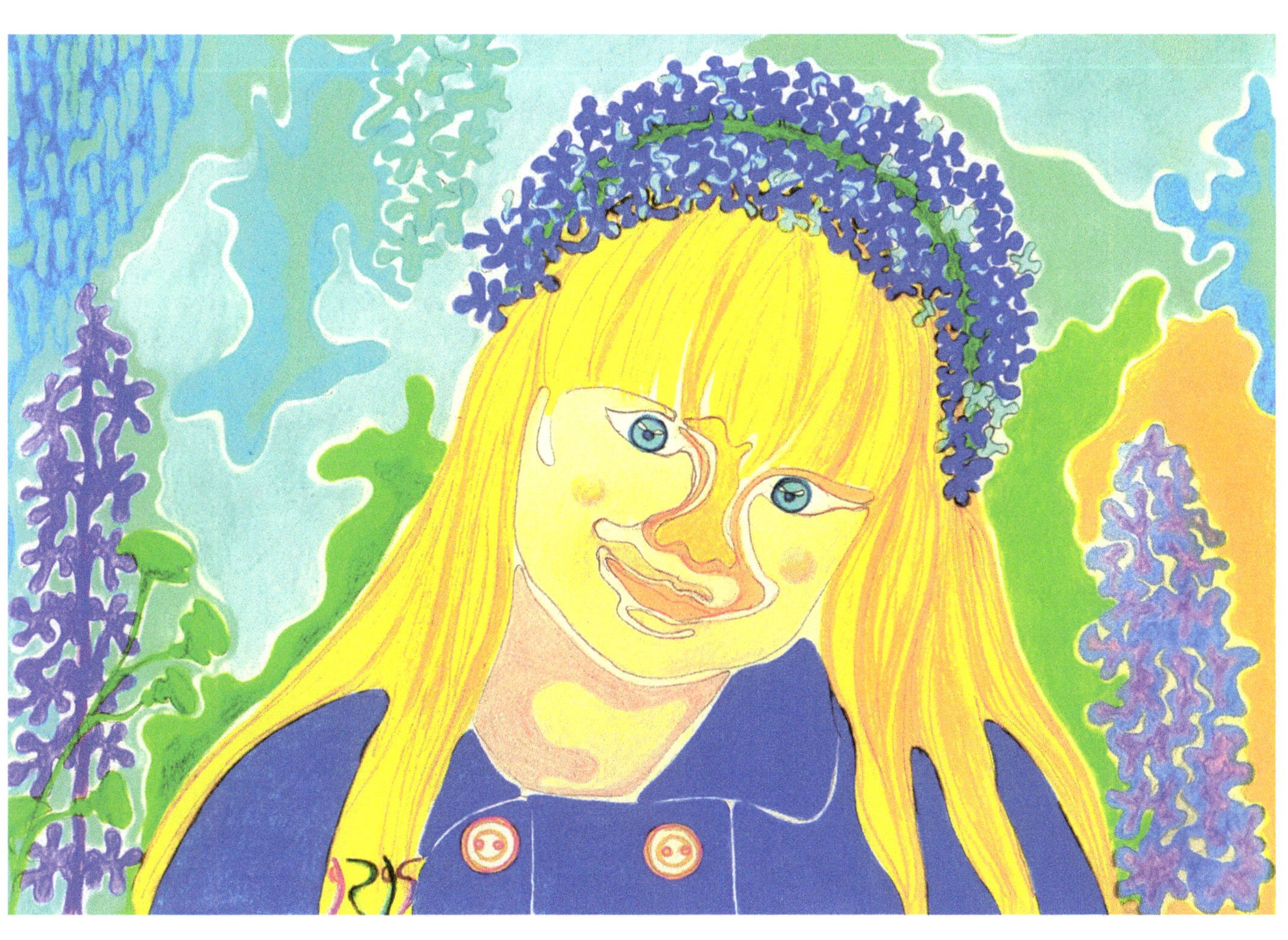

Girl with flower crown.Color pencils.30x21cm.2023

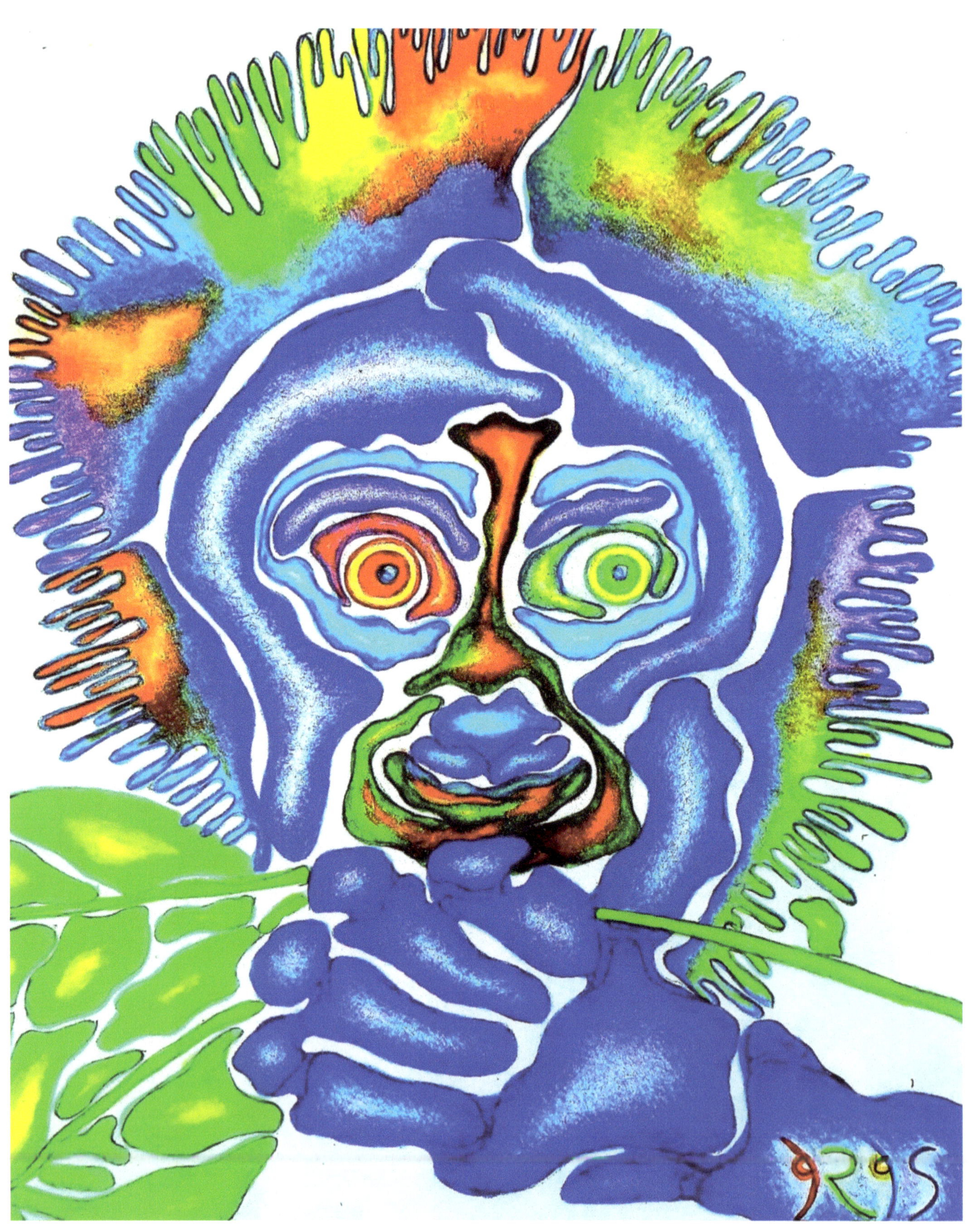

Gorilla Nono.Color pencils.30x21cm.2020

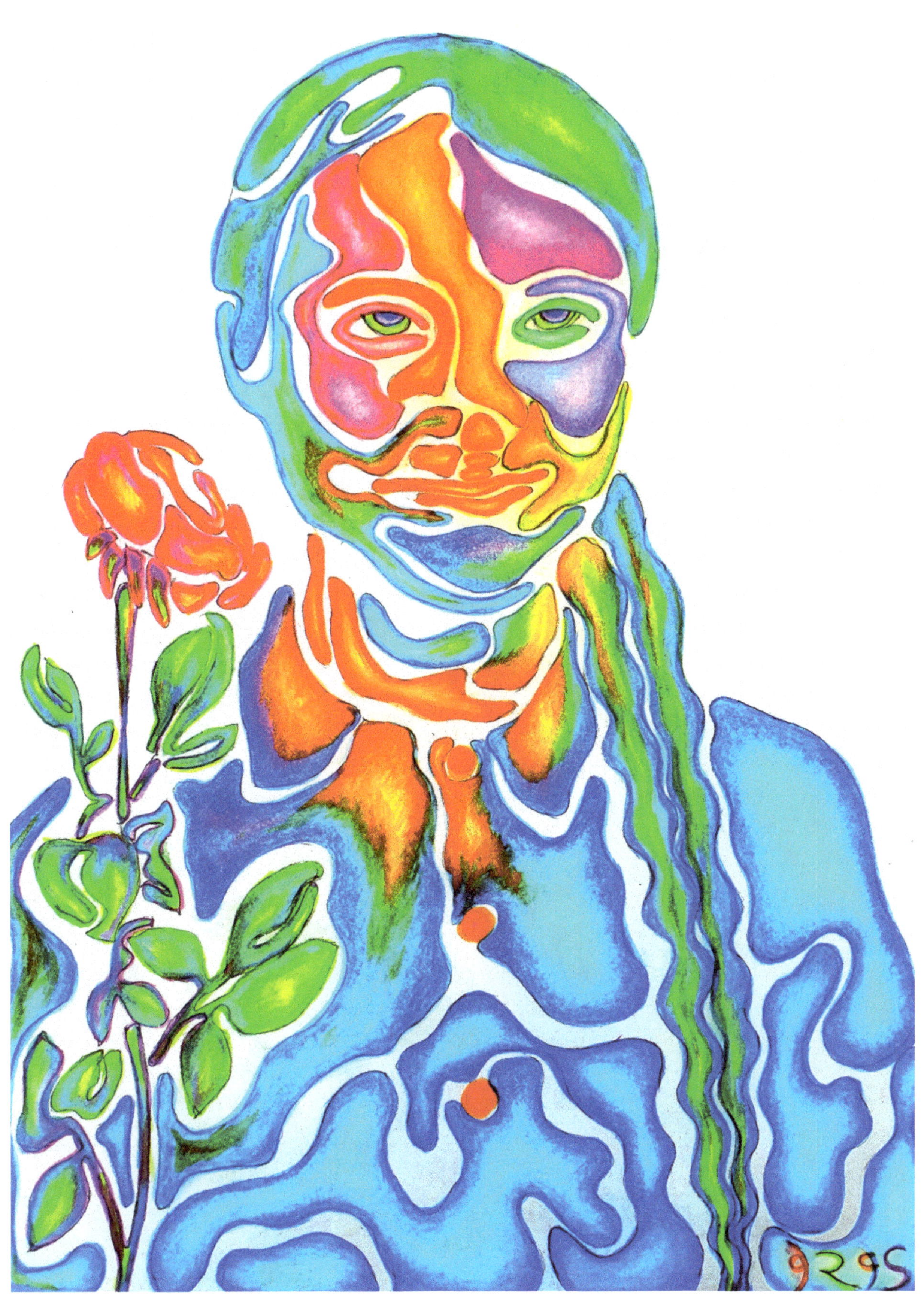

Greta Thunberg. Color pencils.30x21cm.2020

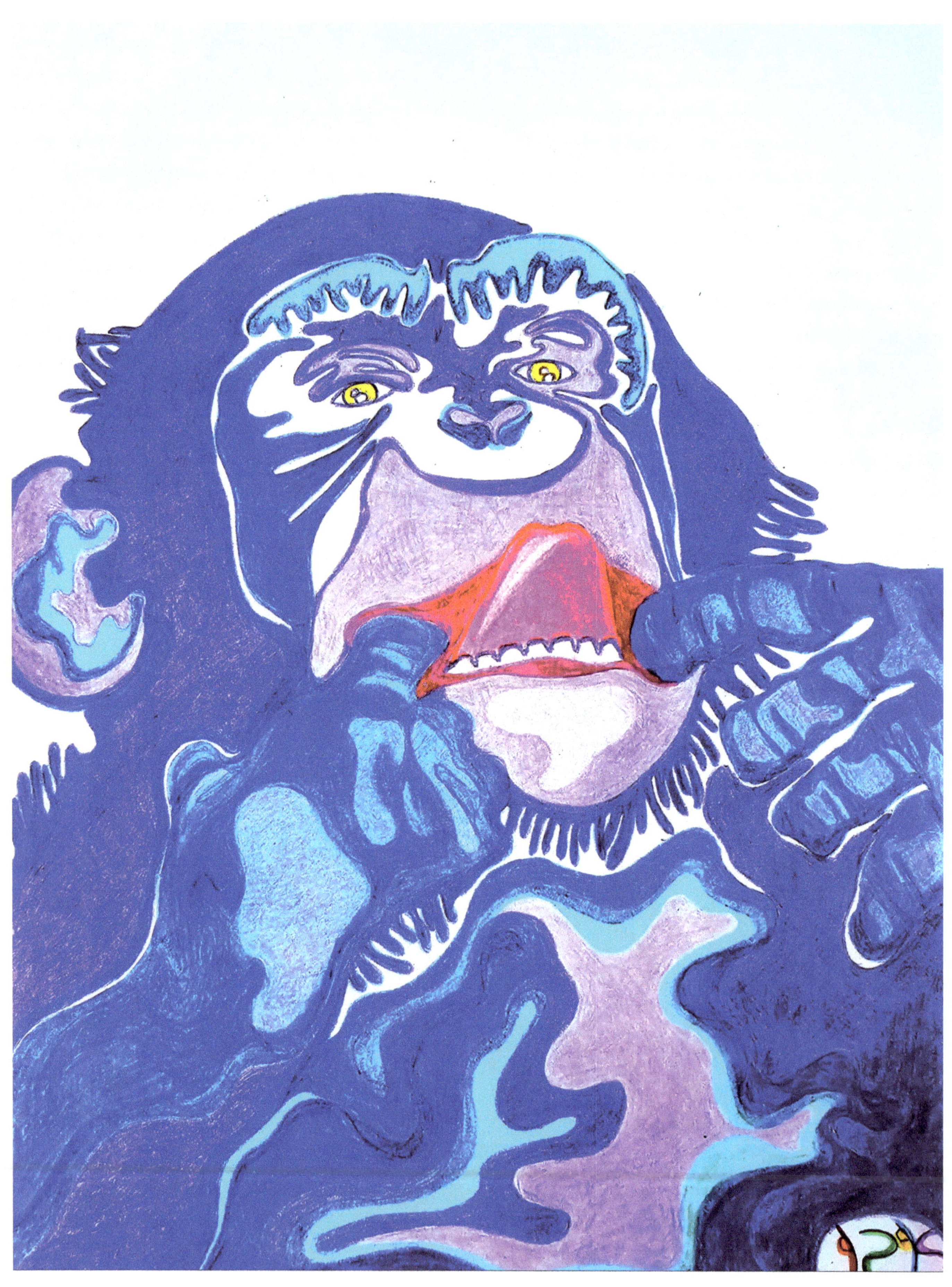

I'm the cutest!.Color pencils.30x21cm.2023

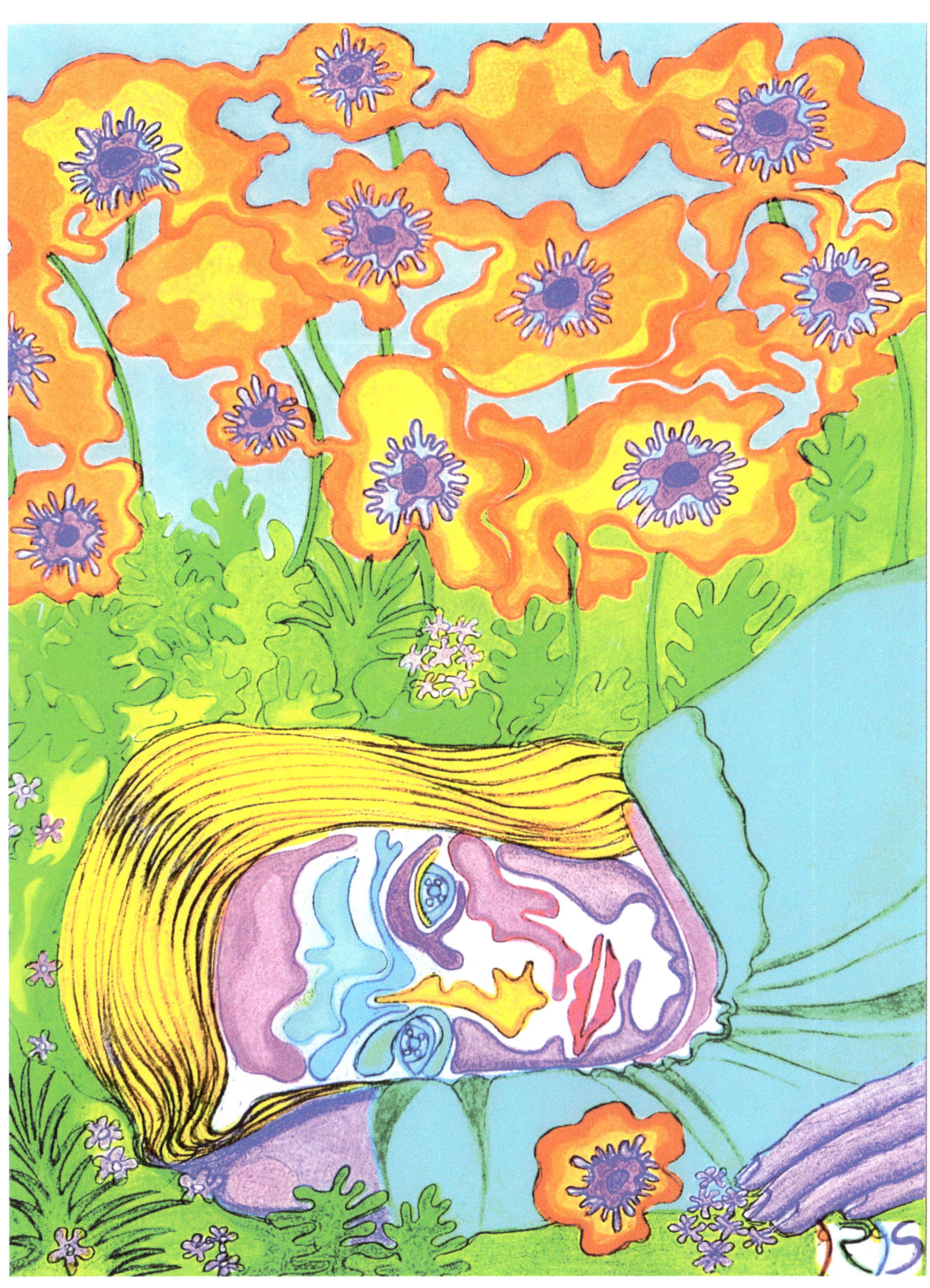

It's a beautiful day. Color pencils.30x21cm.2023

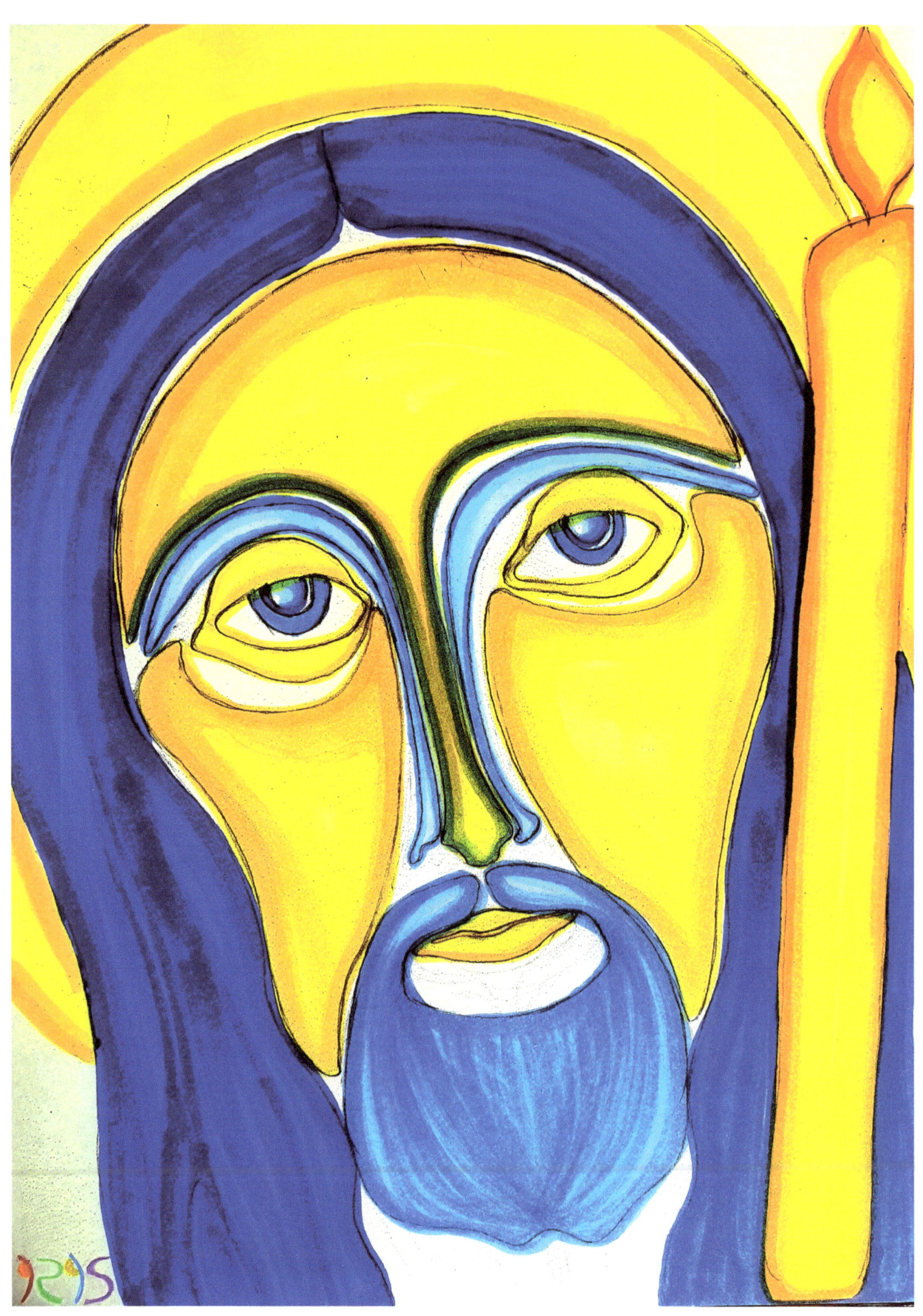

Jesus Christ.Color pencils.30x21cm. 2022

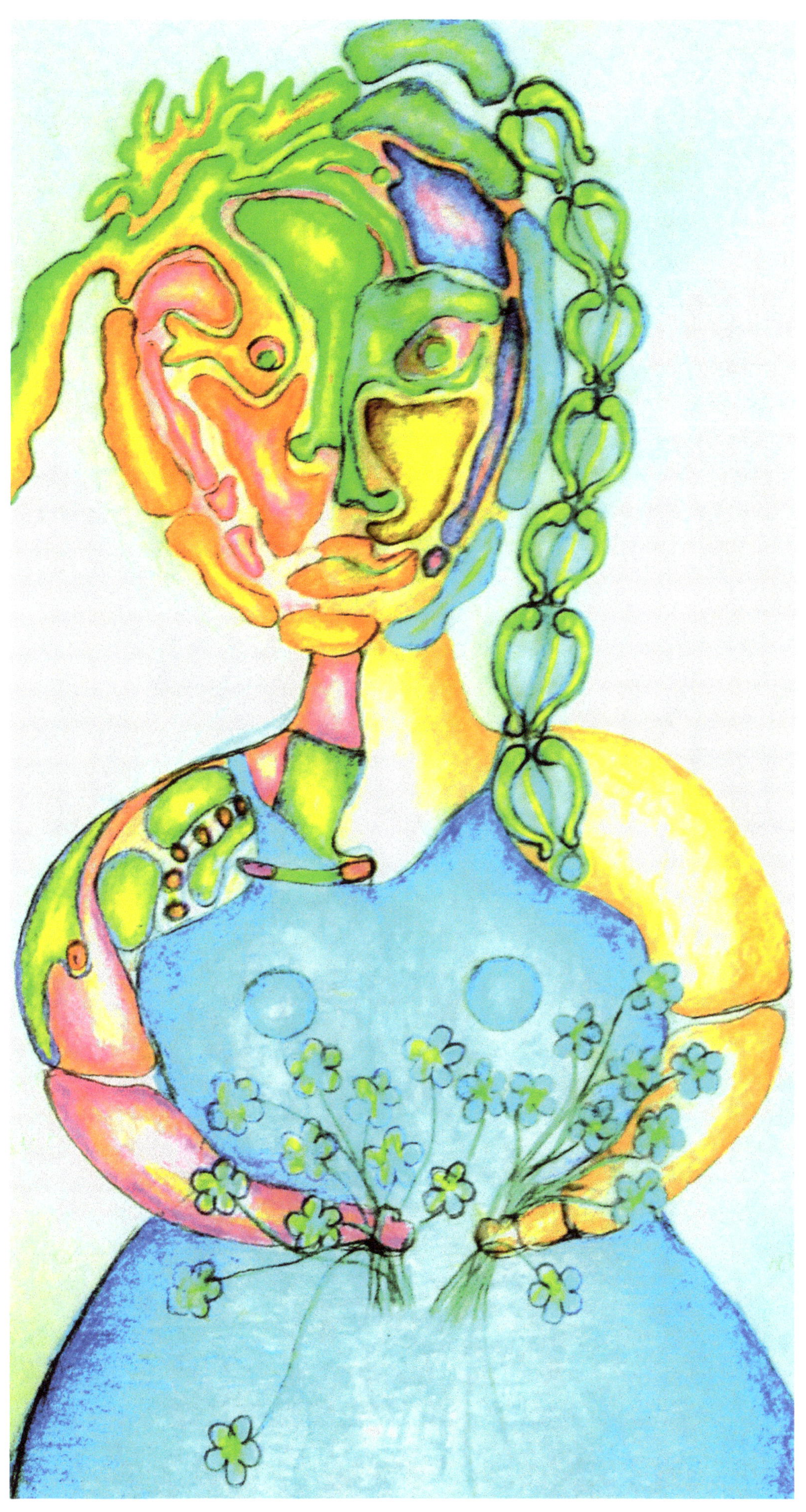

Girl with blue dress.Color pencils.30x21cm. 2018

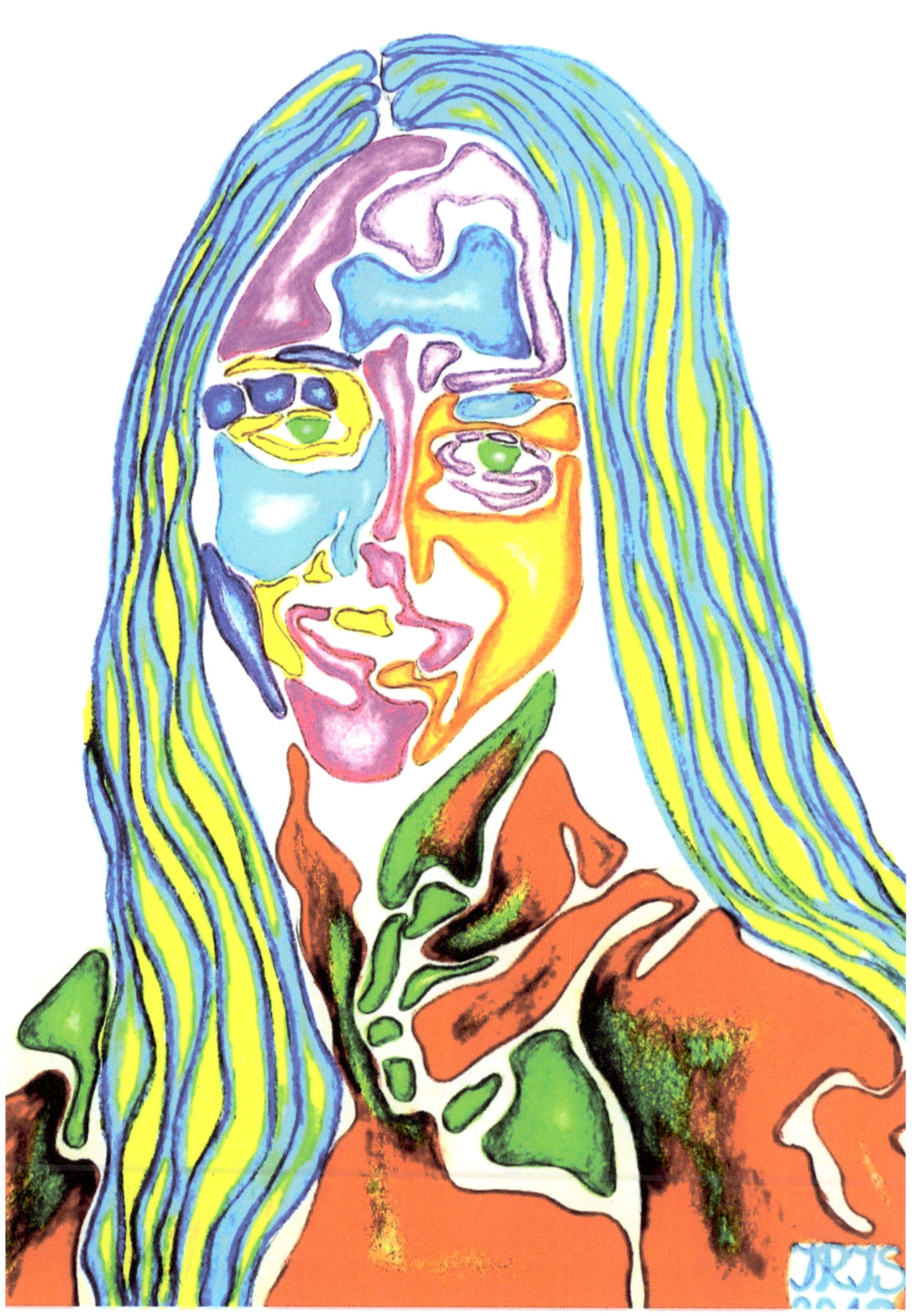

Laura.Color Pencils.30x21cm.2019

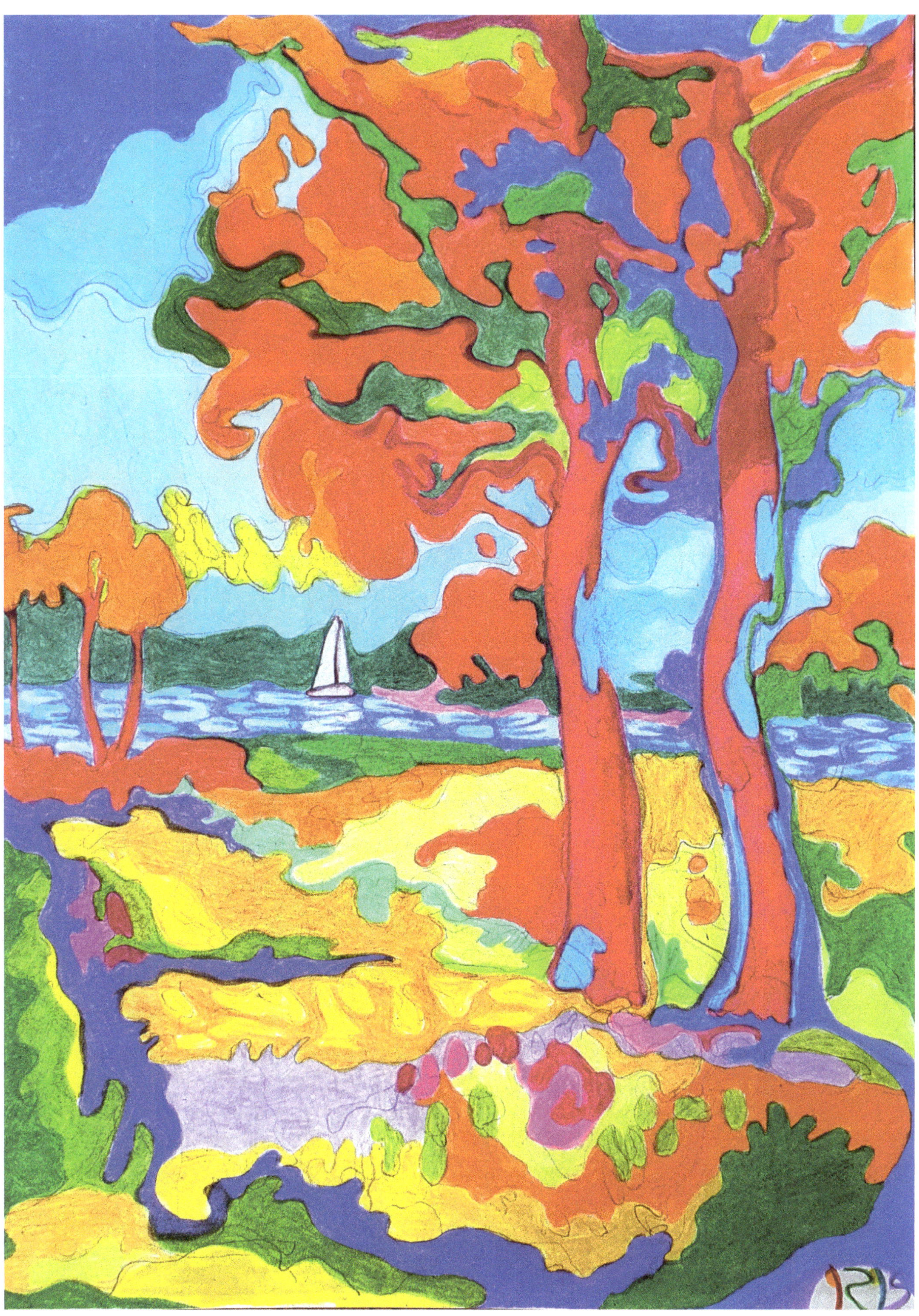

Landscape.Color pencils.30x21cm. 2023

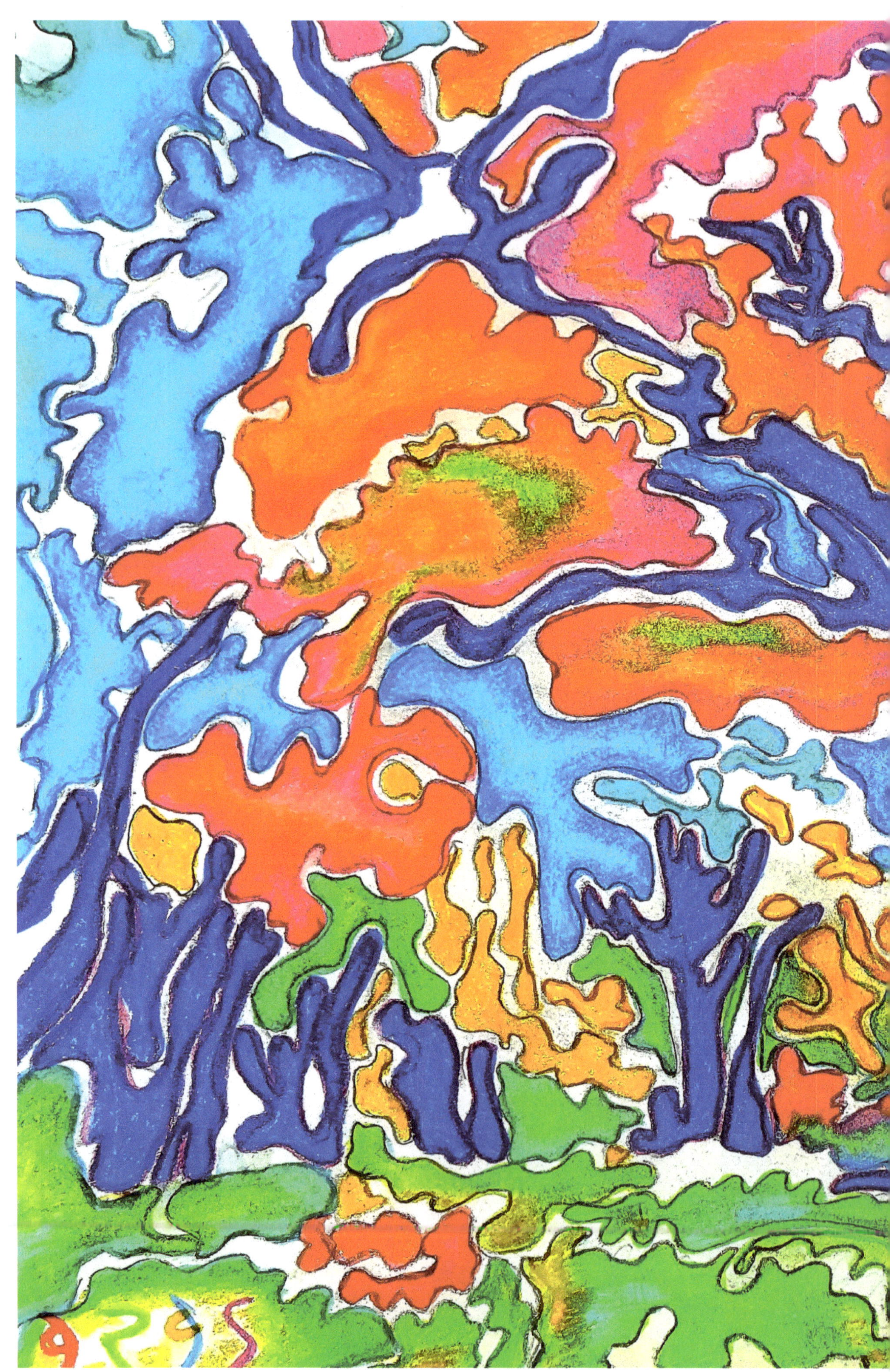

Landscape.Color pencils.30x21cm.2020

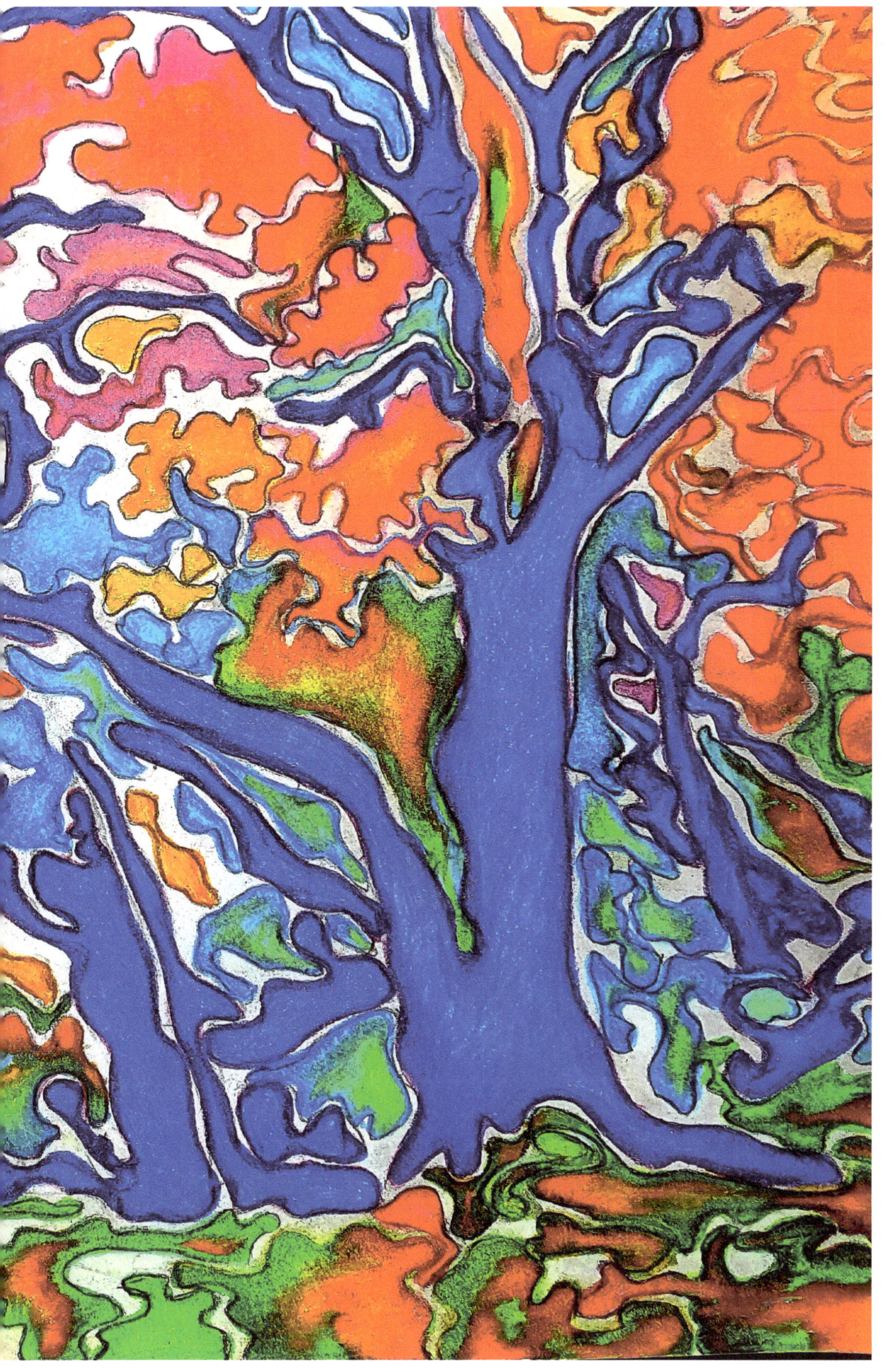

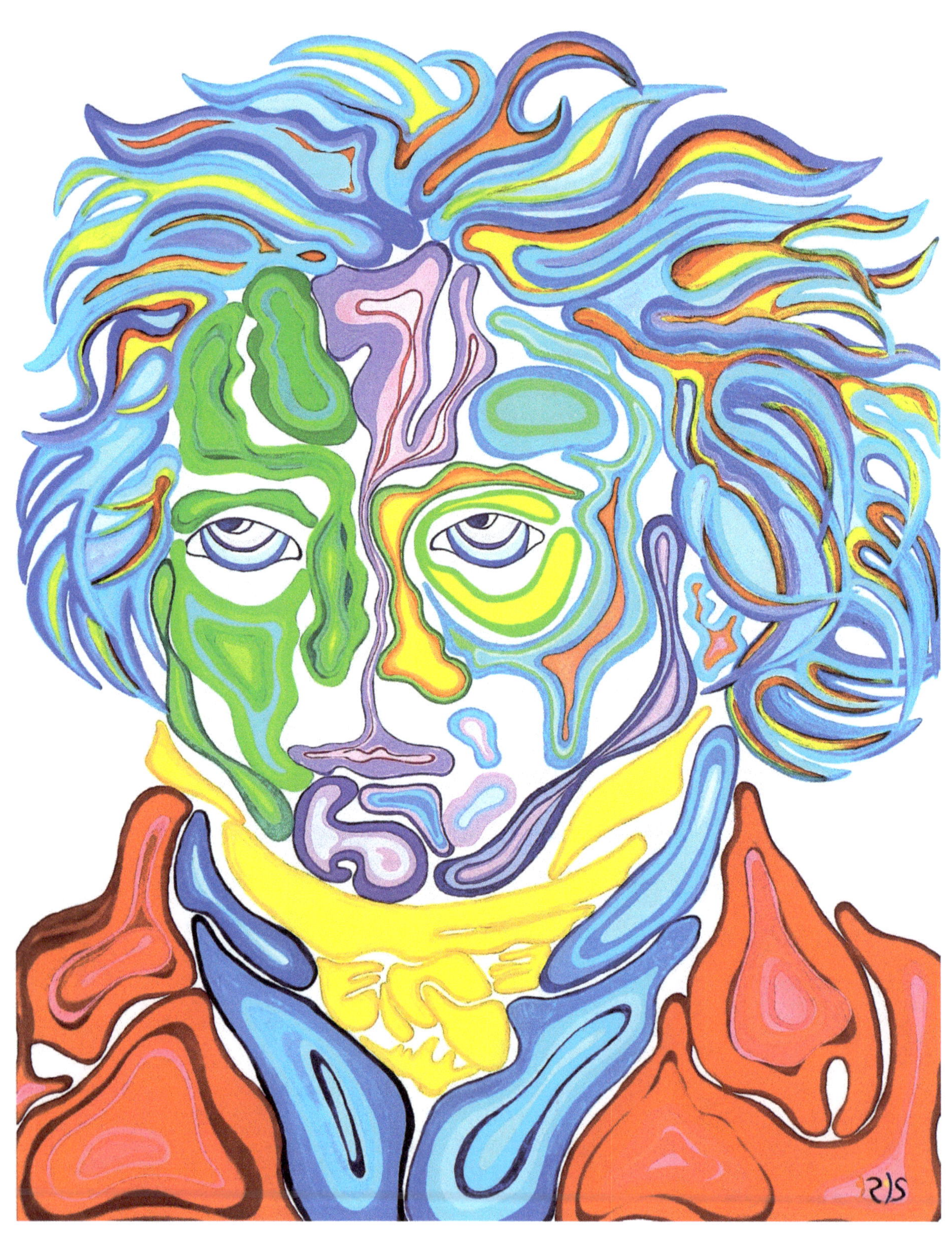

Ludwig van Beethoven young.Acrylic.100x80cm.2020.

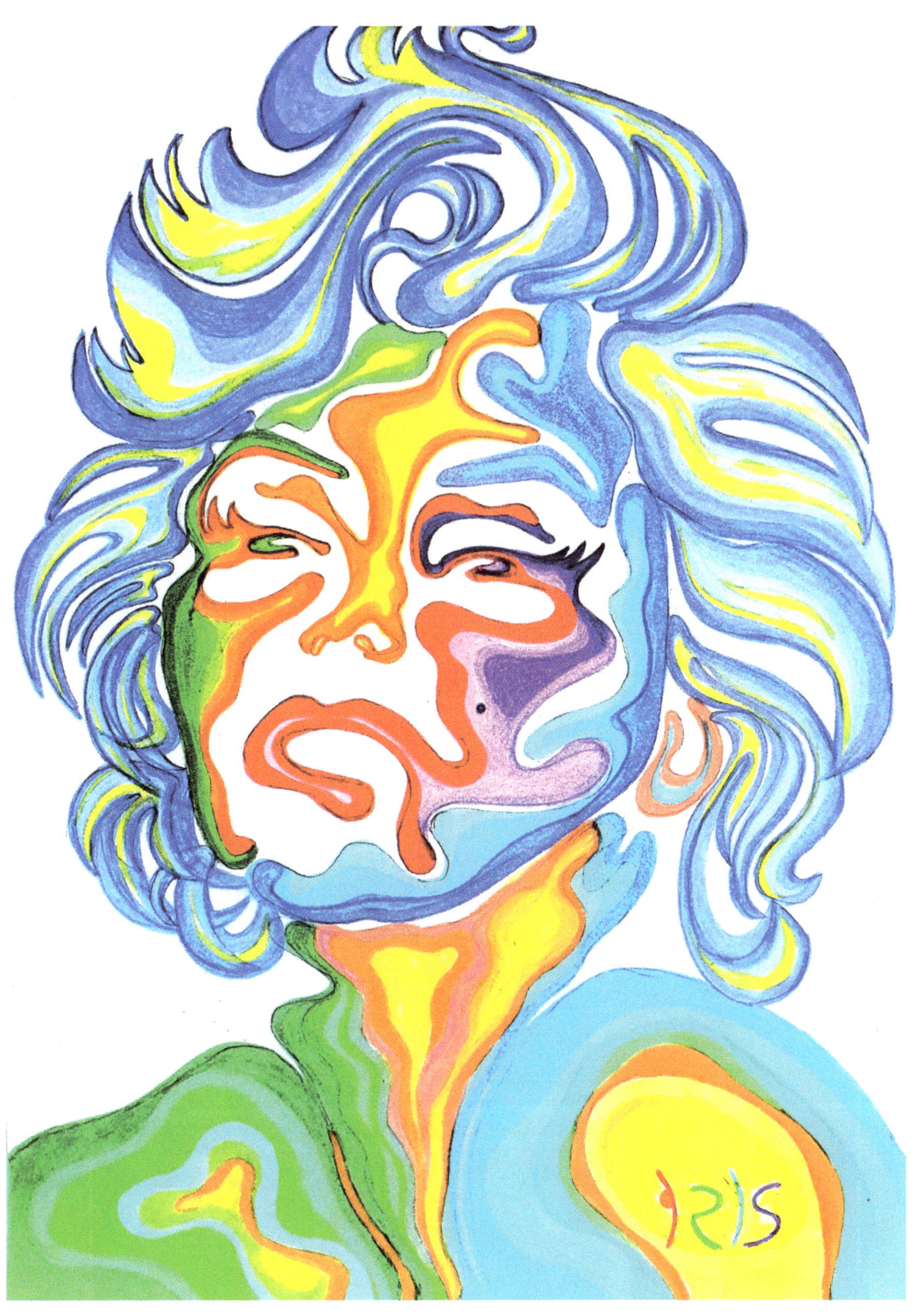

Marilyn Monroe. Color pencils.30x21cm. 2021

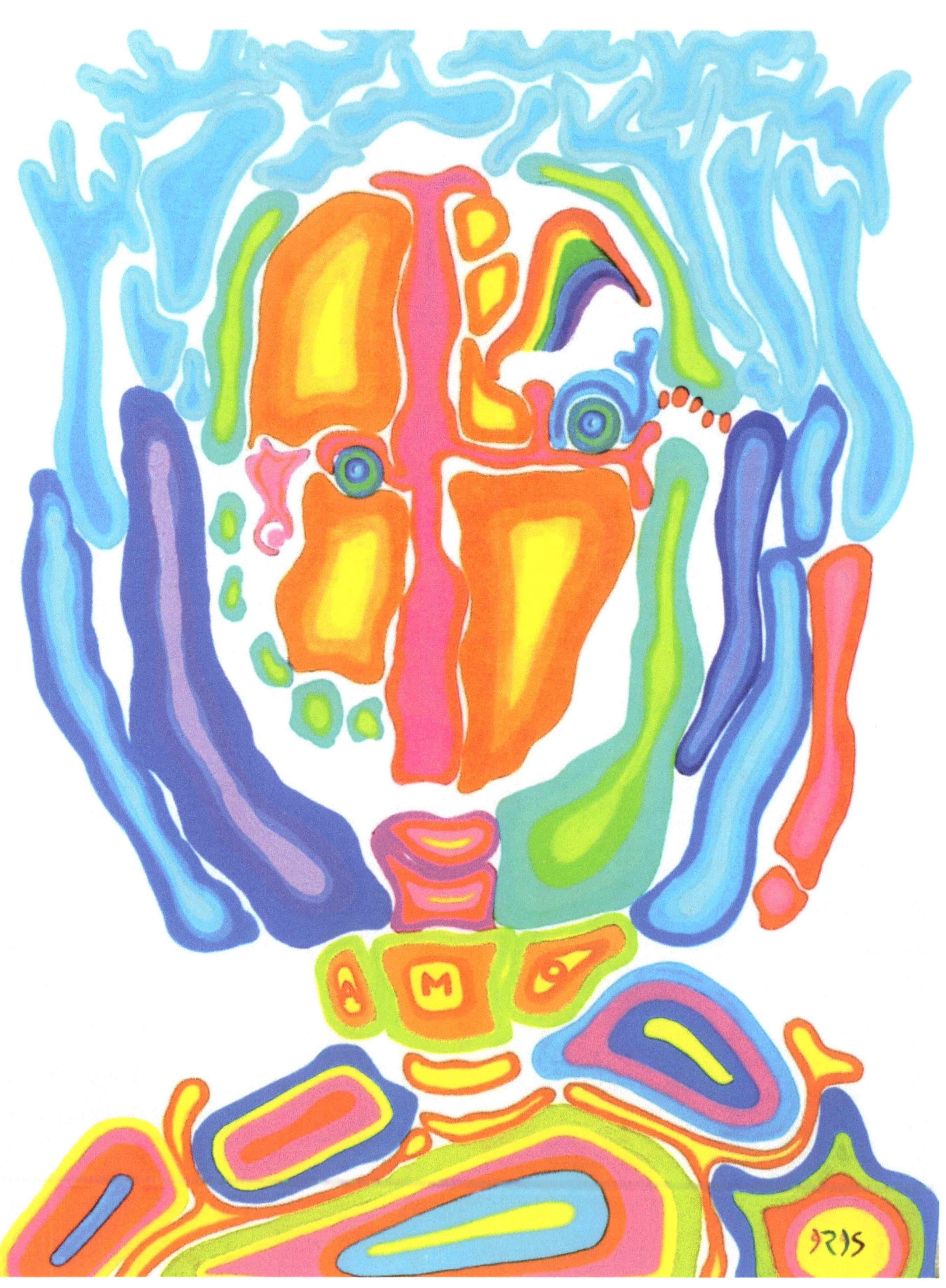

Modern Woman. acrylic.100x80cm.2020

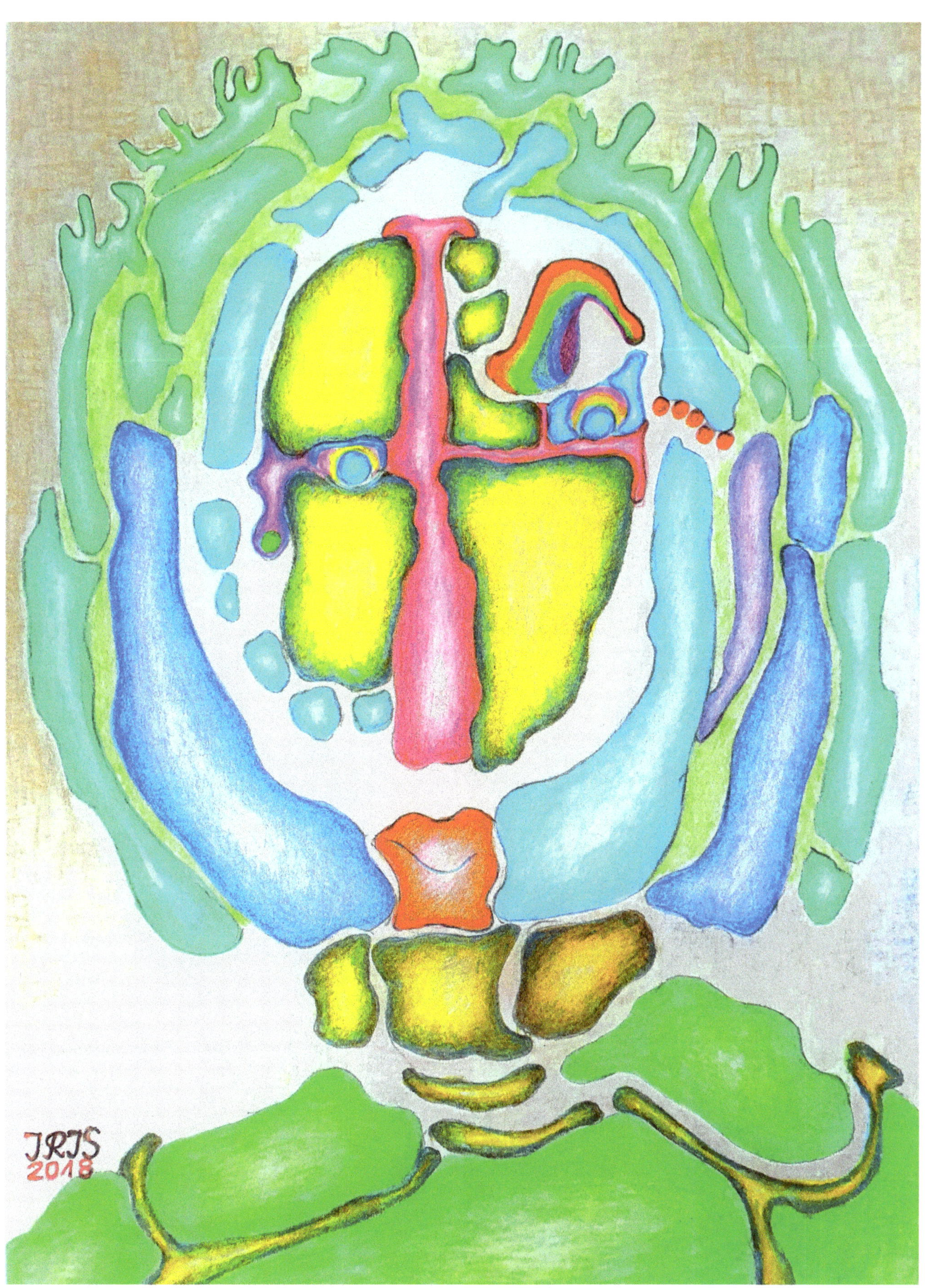

Modern Woman.Color pencils.30x21cm.2018

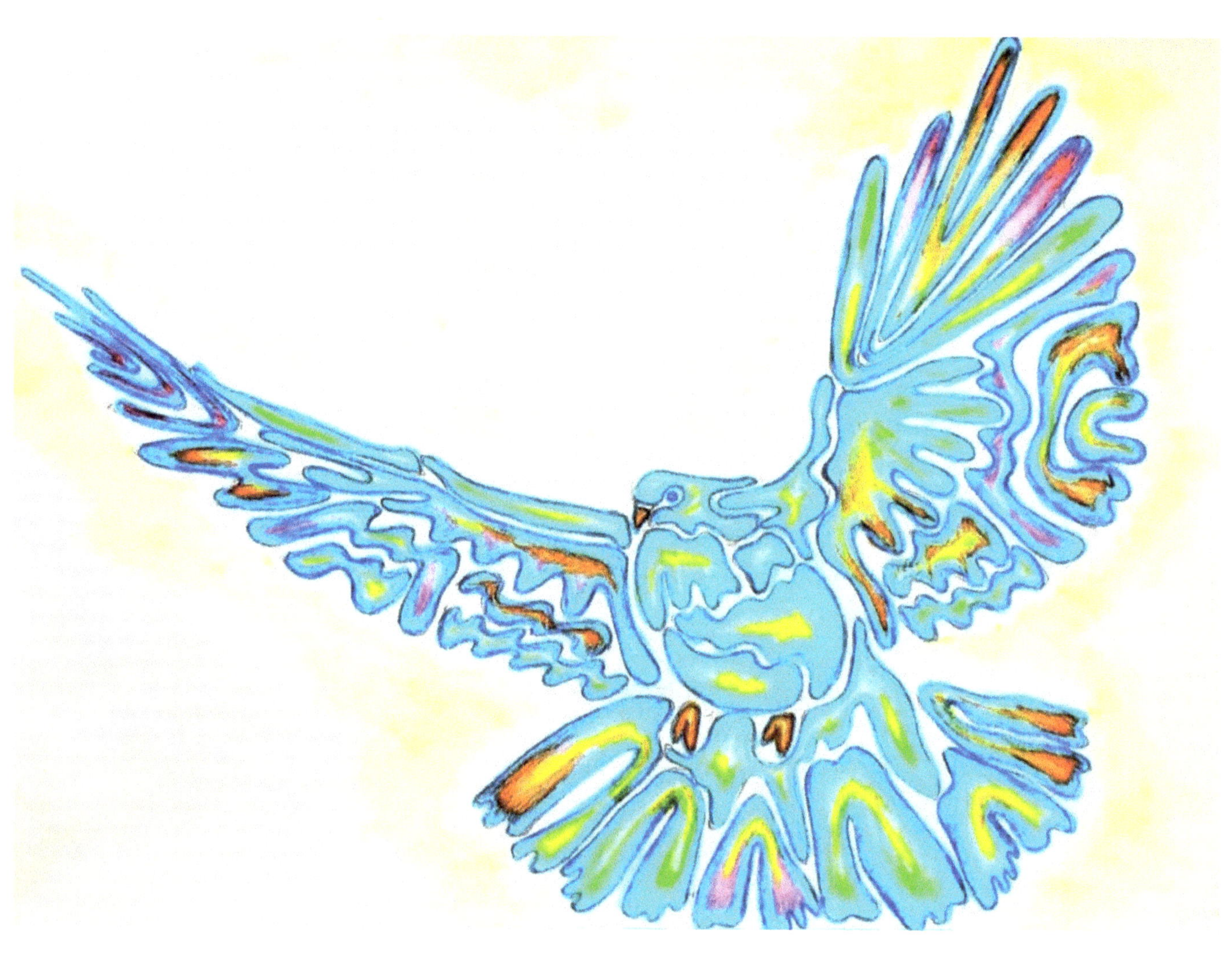

Dove.Color pencils.30x21cm.2020

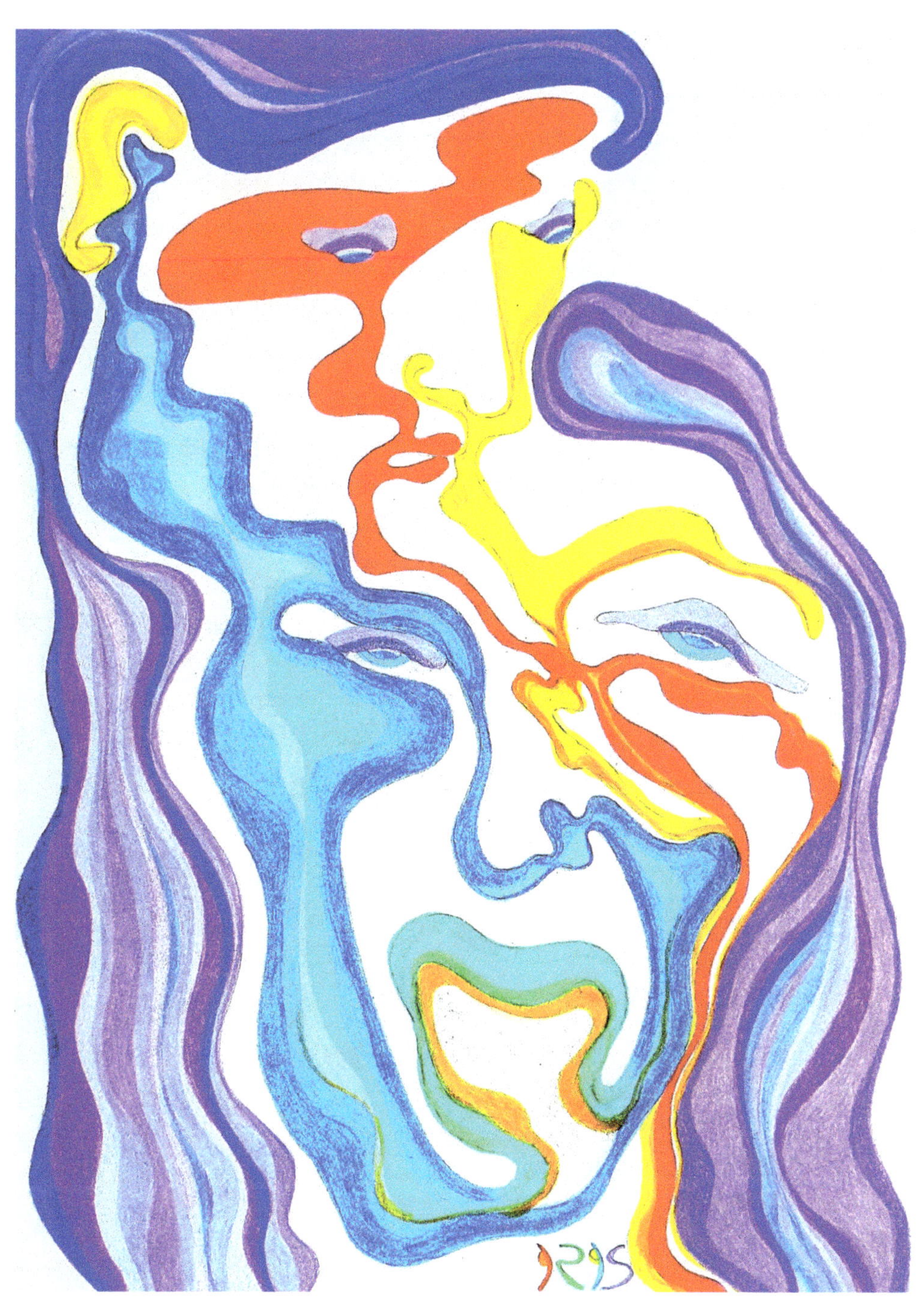

Mother and son.War. Suffering. Color pencils.30x21cm.2023

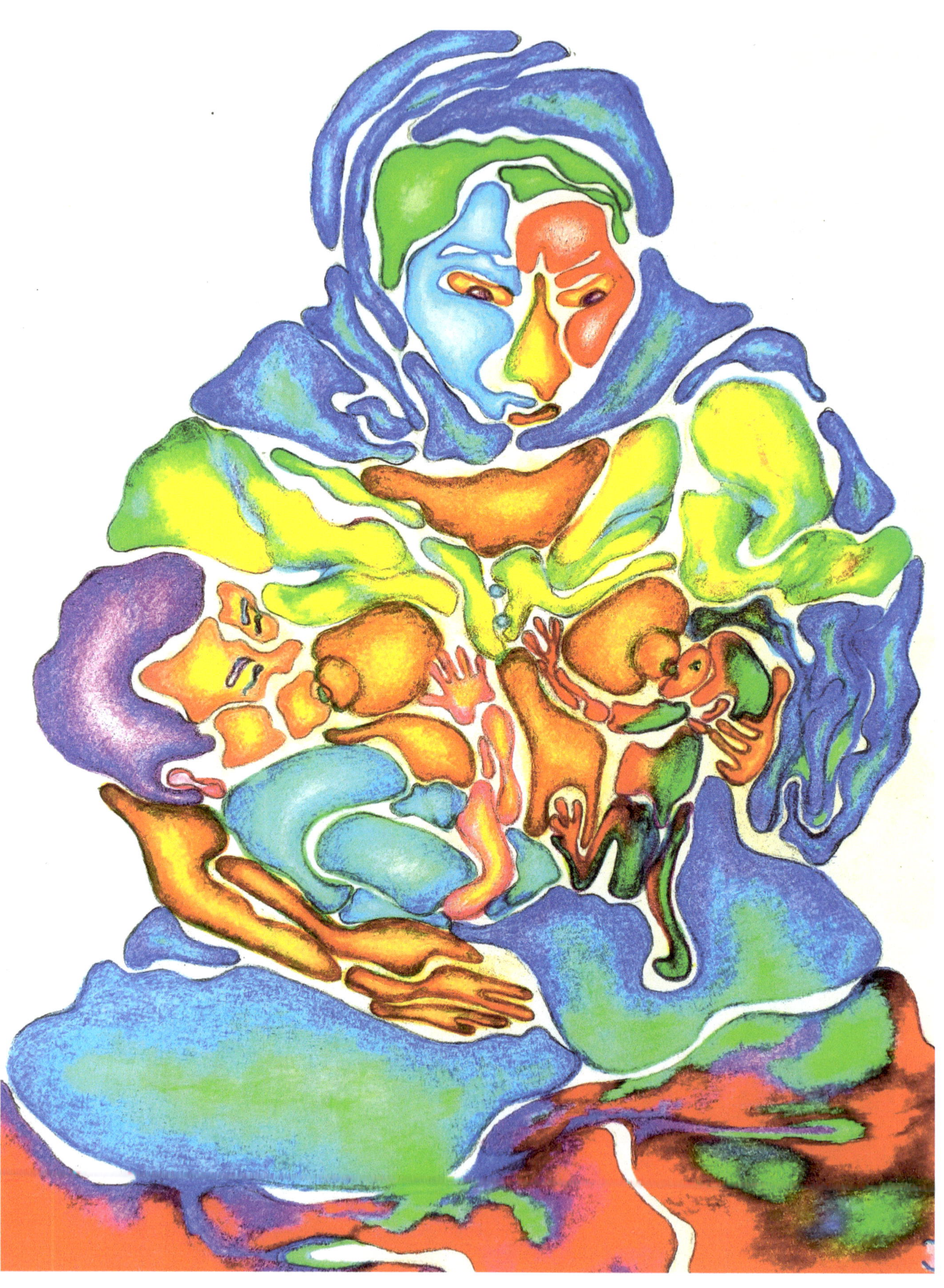

Mother Earth. Color pencils. 30x21cm.2019

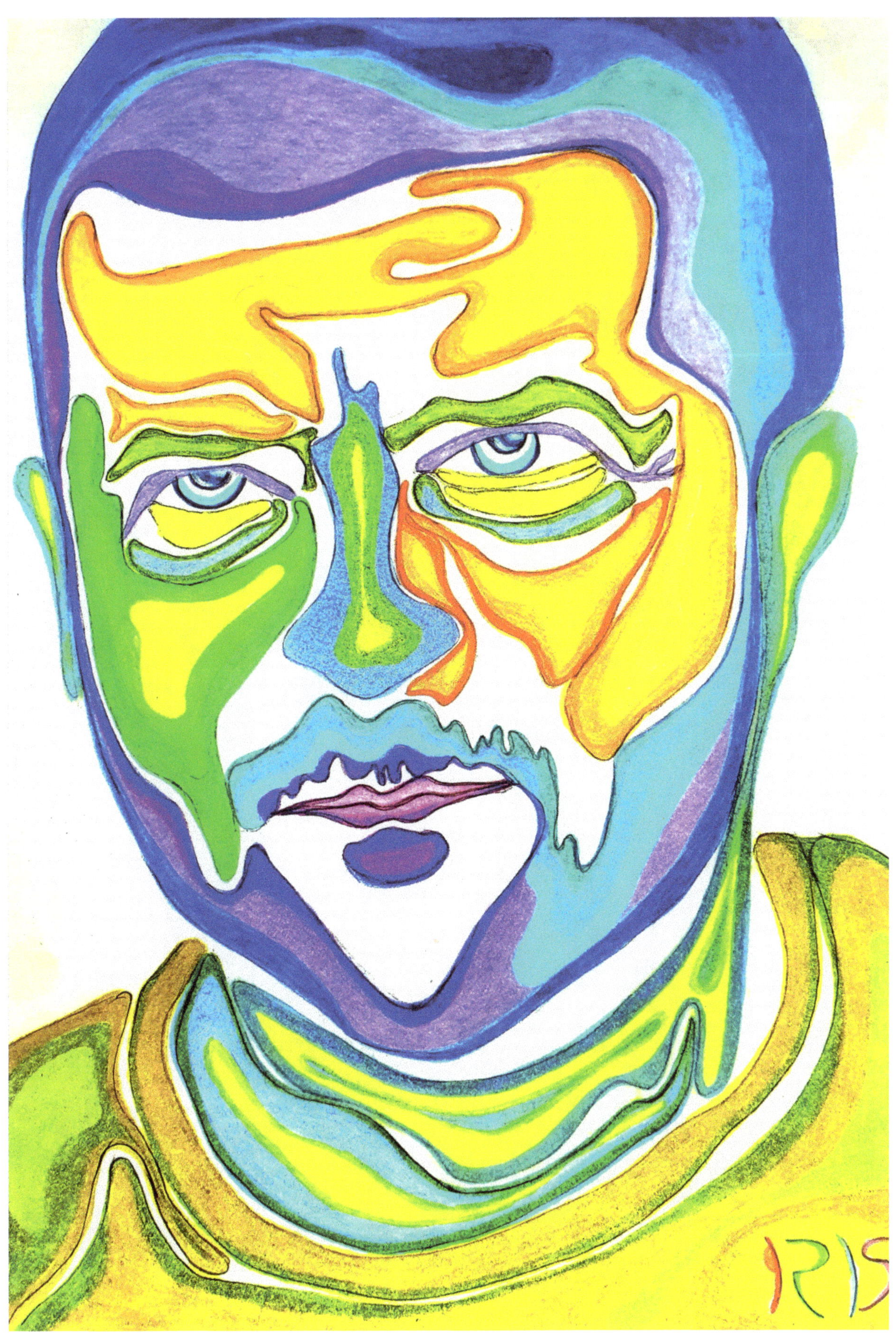

Mr.President. Color pencils. 30x21cm. 2023

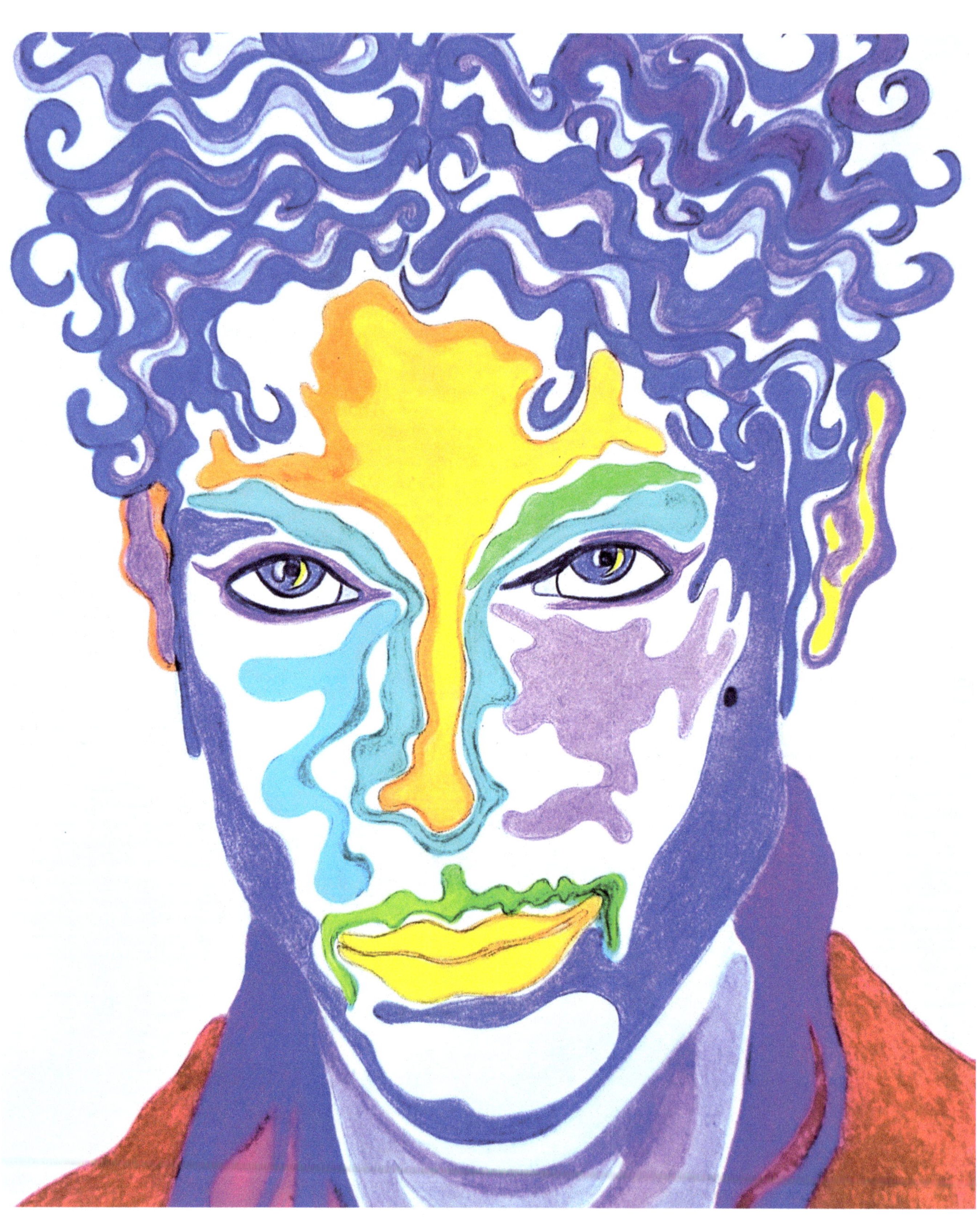

Prince.Color pencils.30x21cm.2024

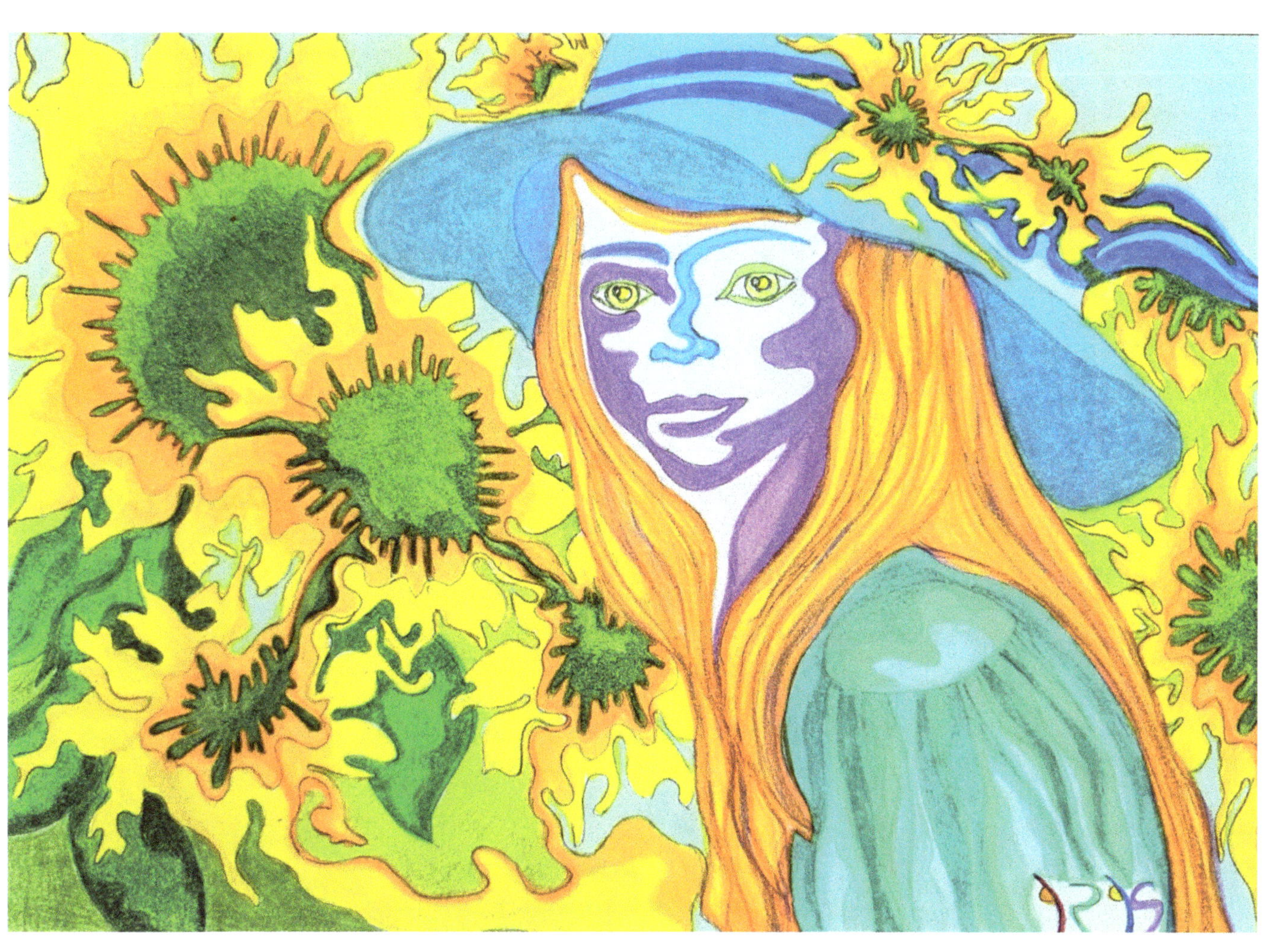

Julia loves sunflowers. Color pencils.30x21cm.2023

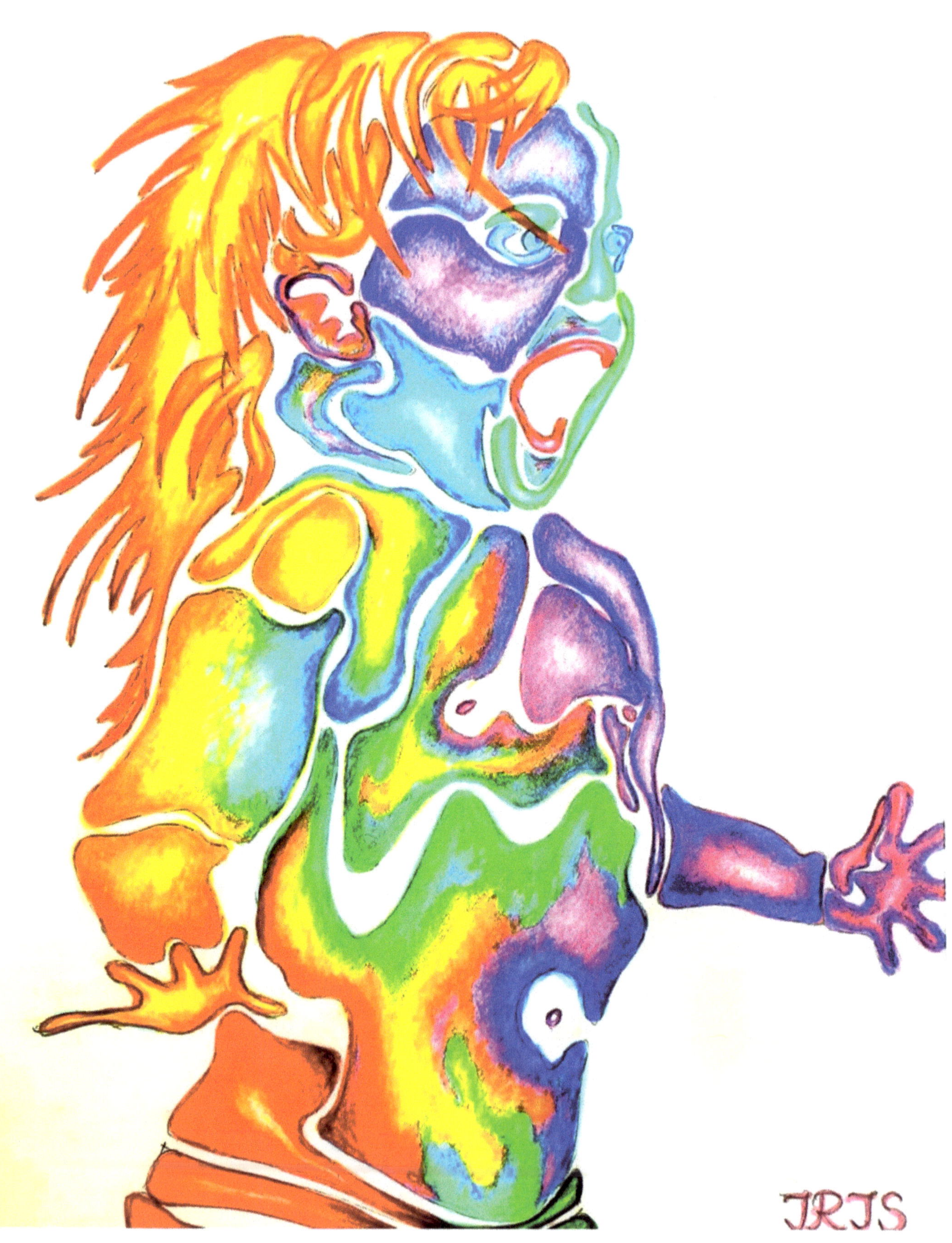

Screaming child.Color pencils.30x21cm.2019

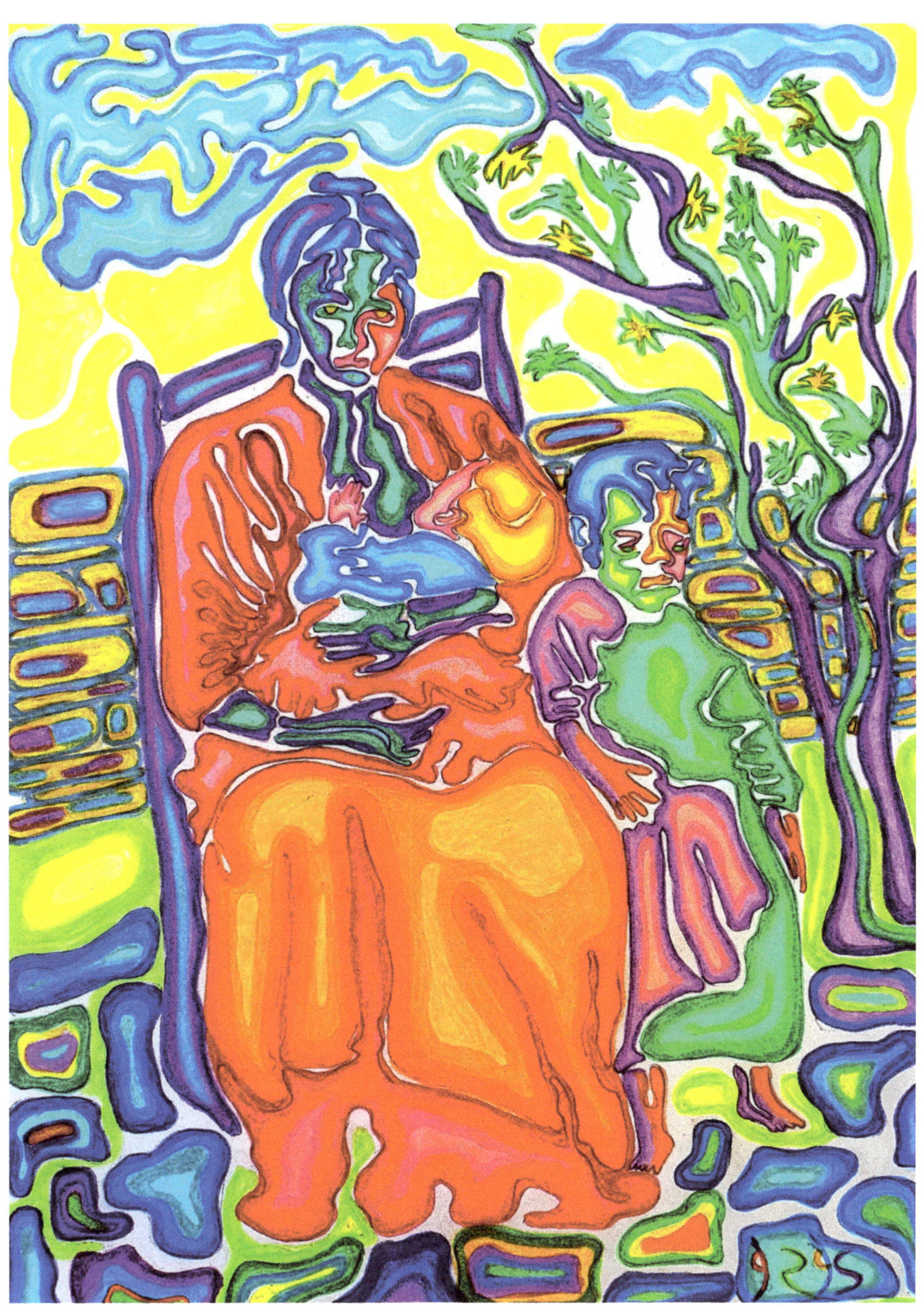

Slave Woman with Children. Black Lives Matter. Color pencils 30x21.2020.

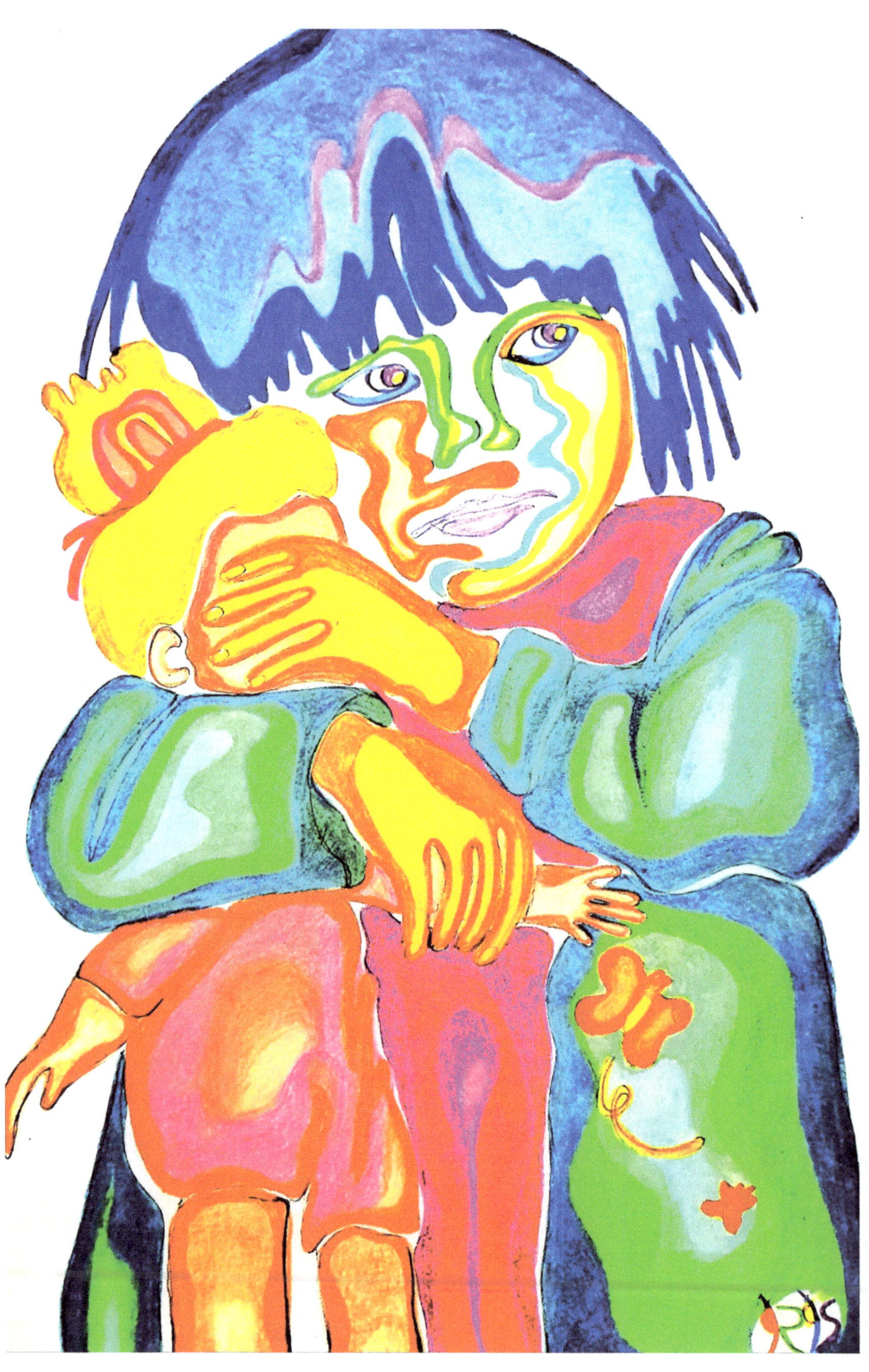

The little girl with the doll.War.Suffering.2022

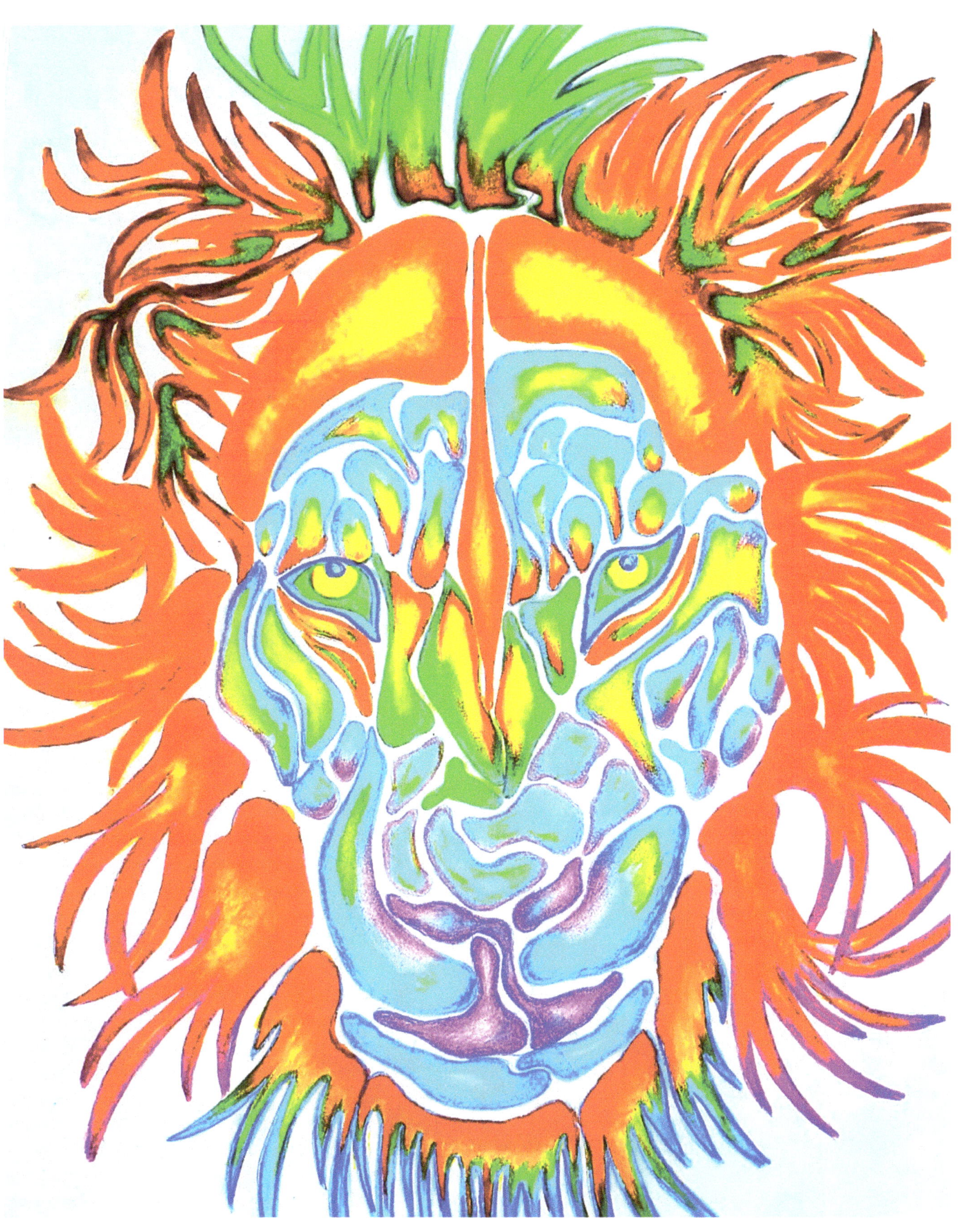

The Punk Lion.Color pencils.30x21cm.2019

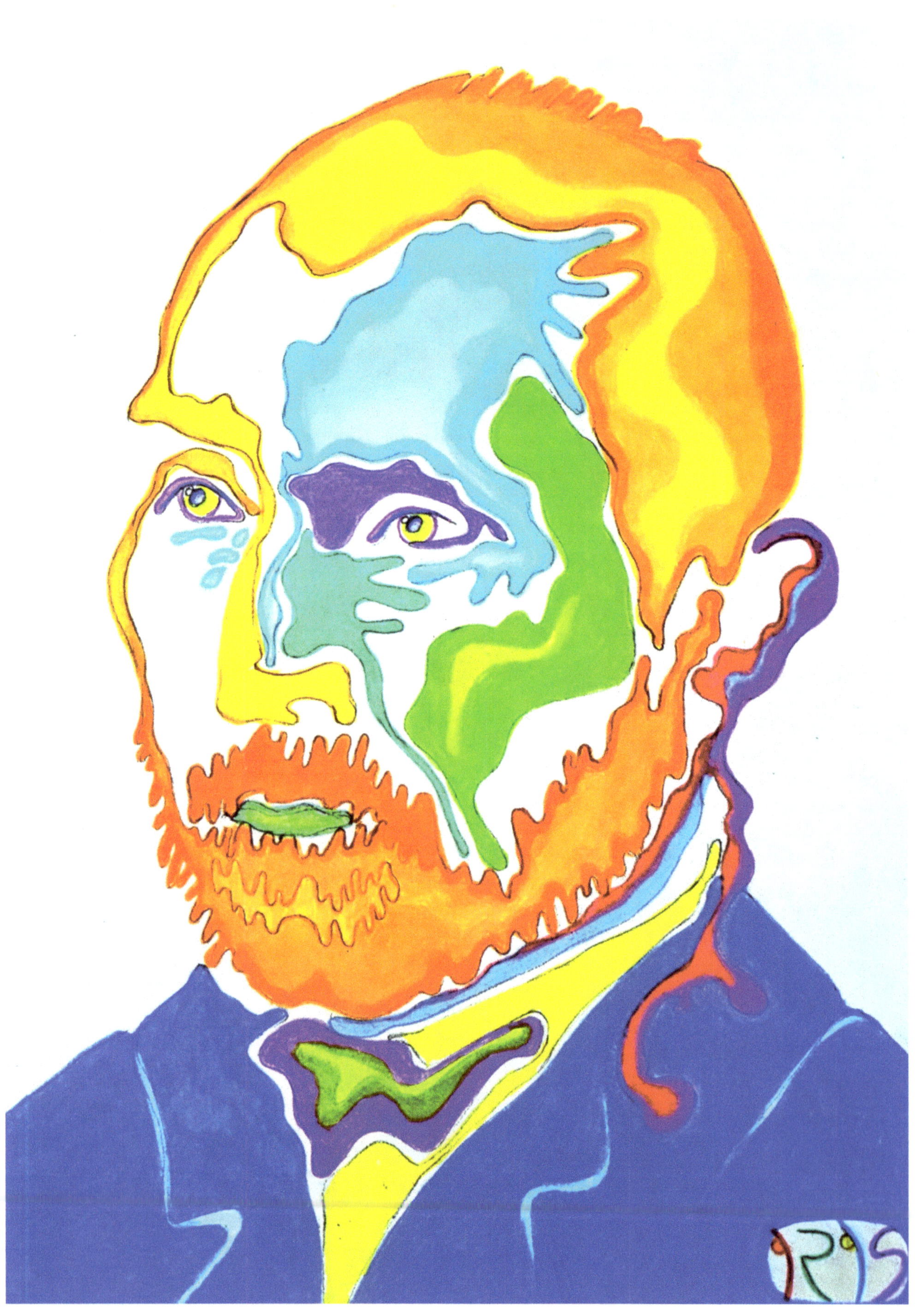

Vincent van Gogh.Color pencils.30x21cm.2023

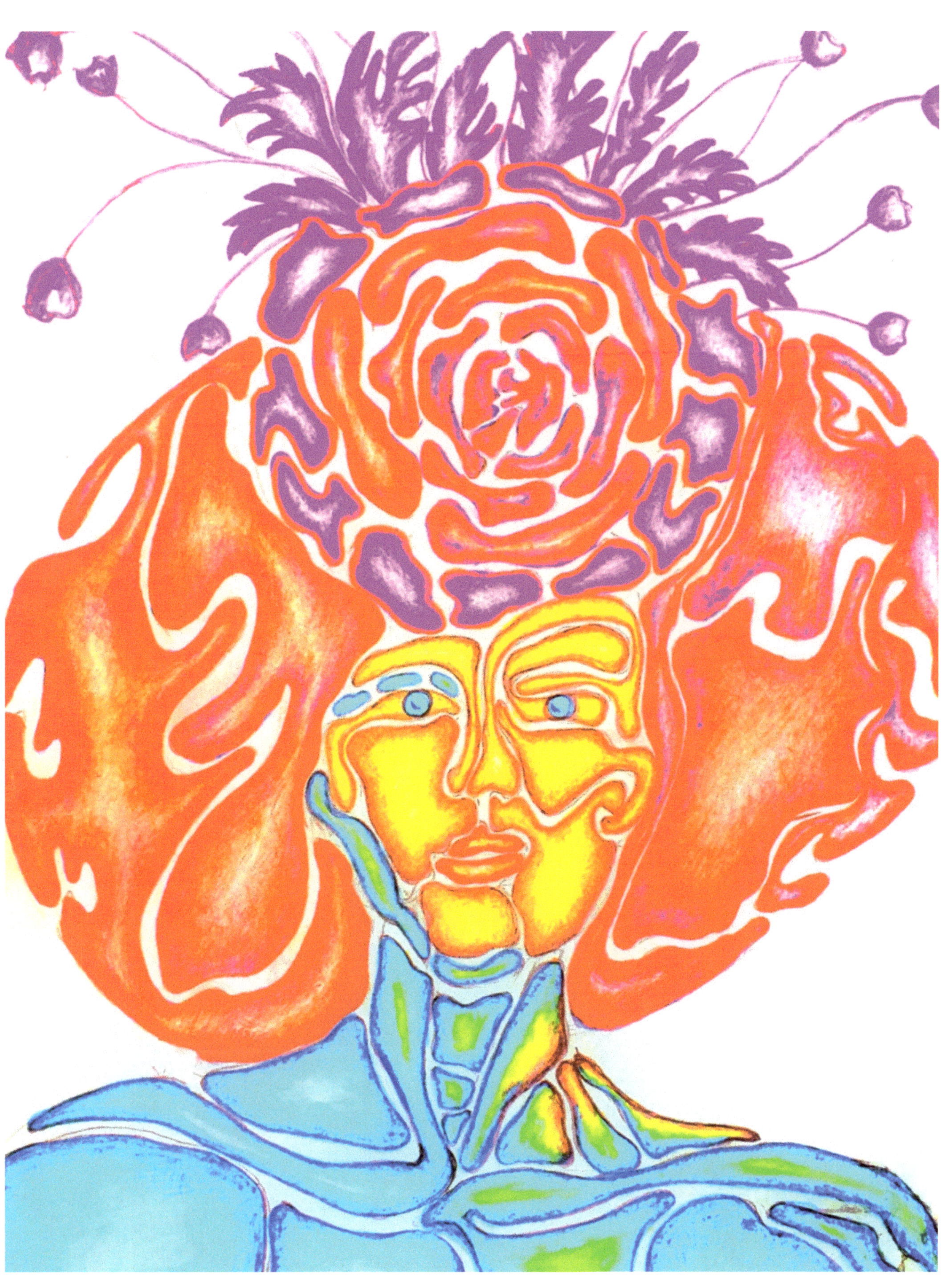

Woman with red hat.Color pencils.30x21cm.2019

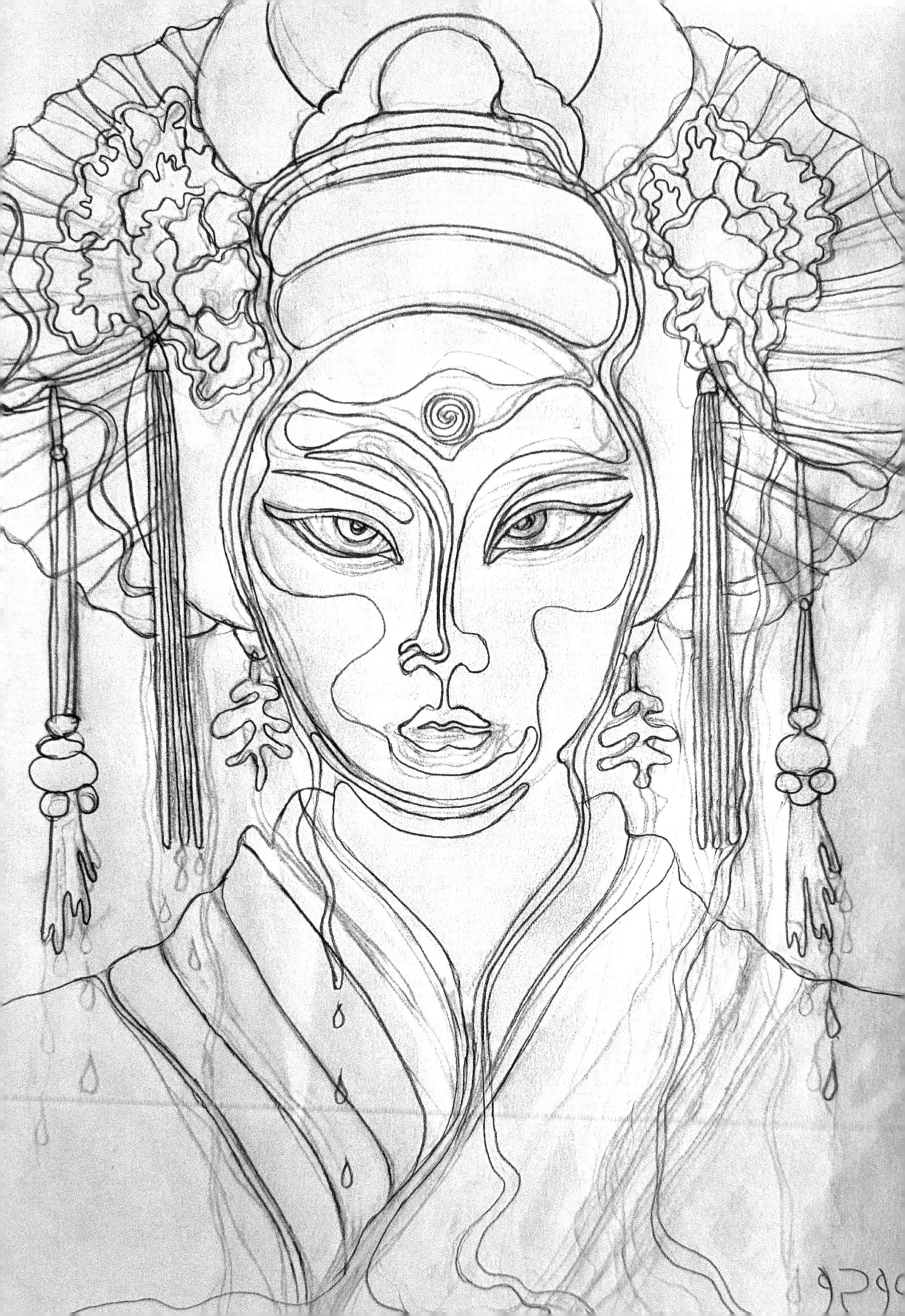

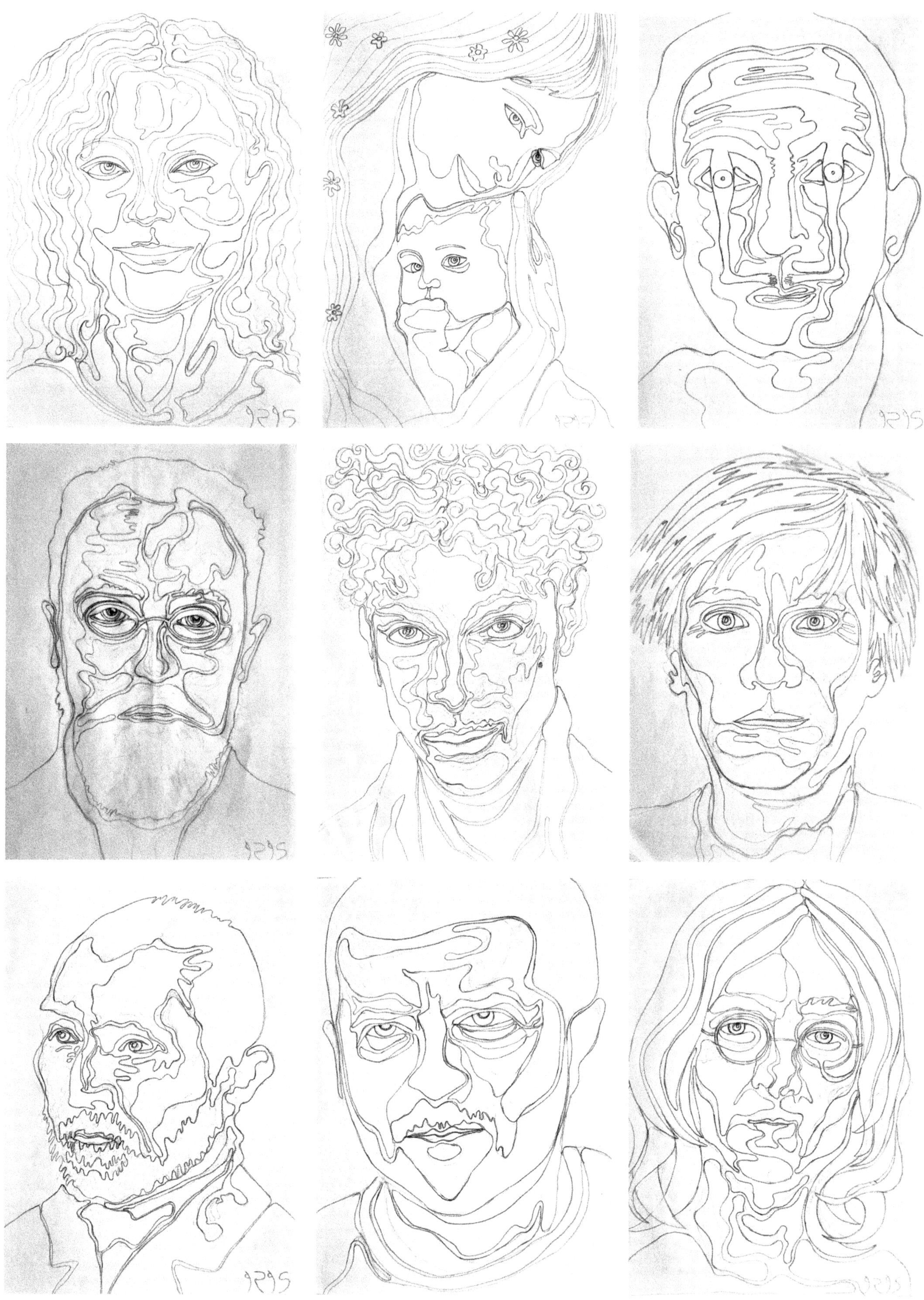

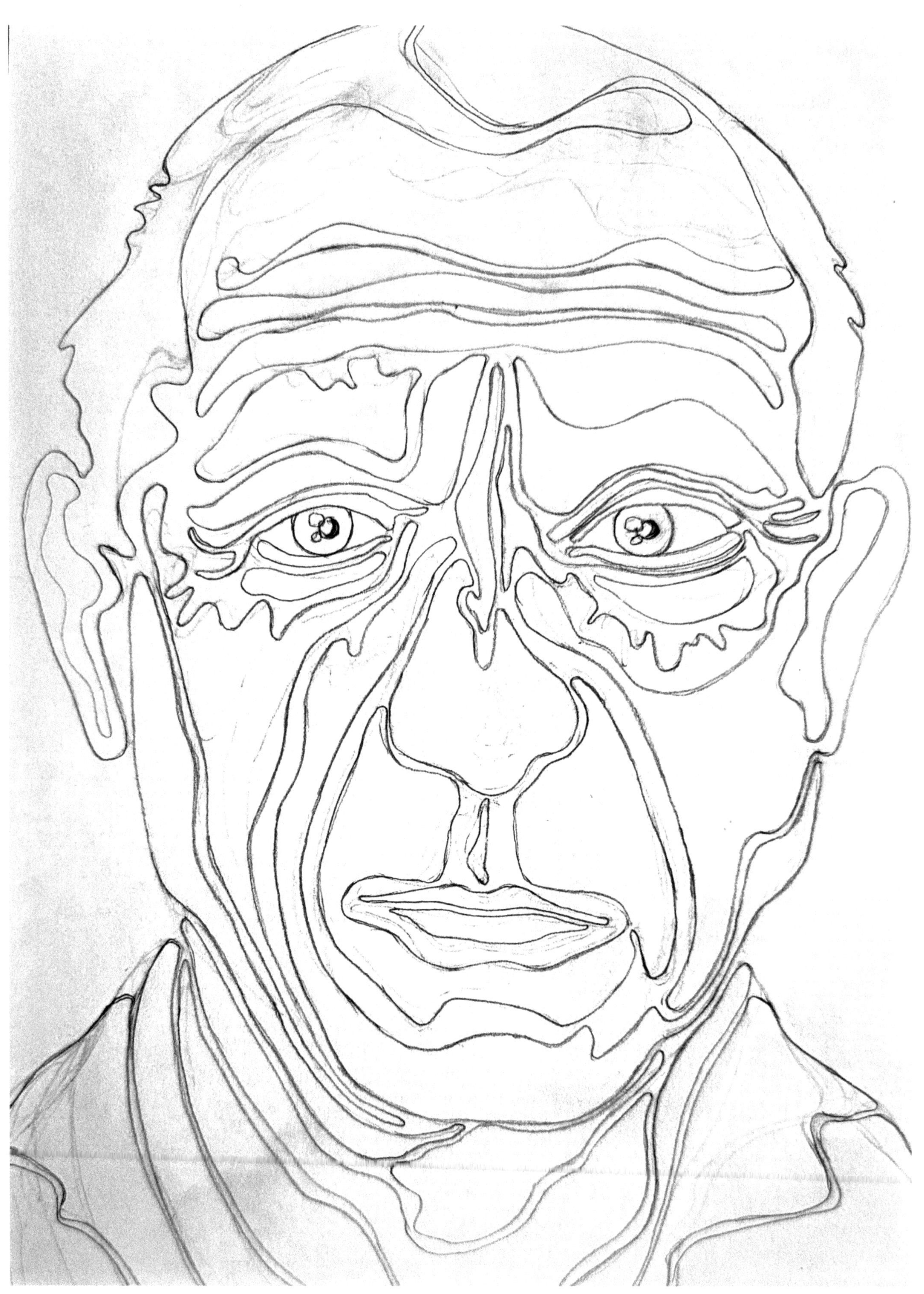

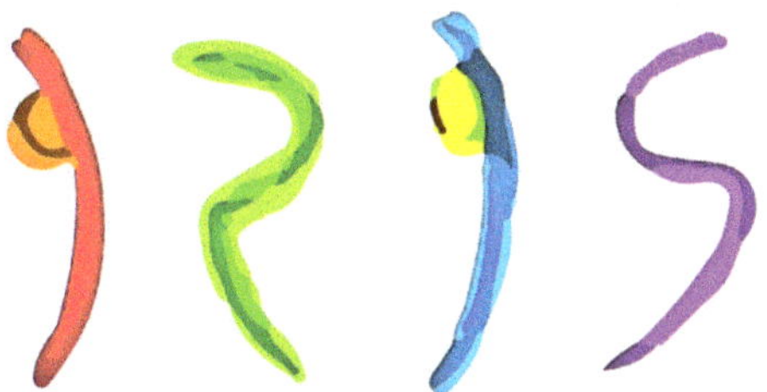

I.R.I.S_ Individual Running Images of the Spectrum. Logo.

IRIS_FLUIDISM, works 2018-2024
Published by Contemporary Art Station

Publisher
ICM Gestora Cultural, SL
Paseo de Gracia 95, 5º-1ª
08008 Barcelona
Spain

ISBN: 978-84-10291-62-1
DL: GR 1270-2024

Library of Congress Cataloging-in-Publication Data
IRIS_FLUIDISM, works 2018-2024 / Contemporary Art Station.
Includes bibliographical references and index
ISBN 978-84-10291-62-1

Printed in Spain, EU.

First Edition, 2024

Publisher's Contact Information:
Contemporary Art Station
contact@contemporaryartstation.com
www.contemporaryartstation.com

**Contemporary
Art Station**